TWO CULTURES OF POLICING

NEW OBSERVATIONS

Howard S. Becker, series editor

The close and detailed observation of social life provides a kind of knowledge that is indispensable to our understanding of society. In the spirit of Robert E. Park, the books in this series draw on an intimate acquaintance with their subjects to make important contributions to the development of sociological theory. They dig beneath the surface of conventional pieties to get at the real story, and thus produce ideas that take account of the realities of social life.

TWO CULTURES OF POLICING

Street Cops and Management Cops

Elizabeth Reuss-Ianni

Transaction Books
New Brunswick (U.S.A.) and London (U.K.)

Library of Congress Catalog Number: 82–7079
ISBN: 0–87855–469–6(cloth)
Printed in the United States of America

Library of Congress Cataloging in Publication Data
Reuss-Ianni, Elizabeth, 1944–
   Two cultures of policing.
   (New observations series)
   Bibliography: p.
   Includes index.
   1. New York (N.Y.)—Police. 2. Police administration
— New York (N.Y.) 3. Police patrol — New York (N.Y.)
I. Title.
HV8148.N5R48   352.2′09747′1   82–7079
ISBN 0–87855–469–6   AACR2

FOR MY RIDING PARTNER

Contents

Acknowledgments

Throughout the eighteen months in which I carried out this research, I worked with, socialized with, observed, and interviewed many police officers in the New York City Police Department. I spent a great deal more time with some than with others, but found everyone very cooperative and courteous. To single out particular officers for special acknowledgment might place more responsibility on them for some of the more critical comments than they deserve. They know who they are and I hope that they know that they have my appreciation and respect.

Professor Howard S. Becker of Northwestern University was a constant consultant and advisor throughout the project and was particularly helpful in analyzing the data and organizing the final manuscript. Mr. Peter Gibbon deserves a special note of appreciation in the preparation of the sections on related police literature.

Without the financial support of the National Institute of Law Enforcement and Criminal Justice, this research could not have been undertaken. I would like to particularly thank the project monitor, Kay Monte-White, and David Farmer, former director of police programs for the National Institute of Law Enforcement and Criminal Justice, for their constant interest and support. Of course, points of view or opinions stated here are those of the author and do not represent the official position or policies of the United States Department of Justice.

As always, I worked closely with my husband and colleague Fritz Ianni and again, as always, it is impossible to know where his ideas and feelings and mine begin and end.

THE POLICE COMMISSIONER ISSUED THE FOLLOWING DIRECTIVE TO THE CHIEF OF OPERATIONS:

"Tomorrow evening at approximately 2000 hours, Haley's Comet will be visible in this area, an event which occurs only once every 75 years. Have the men assemble in front of the station house in uniform and I will explain this rare phenomenon to them. In case of rain we will not be able to see anything, so assemble the men in the sitting room and I will show them films of it."

THE CHIEF OF OPERATIONS DIRECTED THE AREA COMMANDER:

"By order of the Police Commissioner: Tomorrow at 2000 hours Haley's Comet will appear above the station house. If it rains, fall the men out in uniform and then march to the sitting room where the rare phenomenon will take place, something which occurs only once every 75 years."

THE AREA COMMANDER ORDERED THE PRECINCT COMMANDING OFFICER:

"By order of the Police Commissioner in uniform at 2000 hours tomorrow evening the phenomenal Halley's Comet will appear in the sitting room. In case of rain in front of the station house, the Police Commissioner will give another order, something which occurs once every 75 years."

THE PRECINCT COMMANDING OFFICER ISSUED THE FOLLOWING ORDER TO THE ADMINISTRATIVE LIEUTENANT:

"Tomorrow at 2000 hours, the Police Commissioner will appear in front of the station house with Halley's Comet, something which happens every 75 years. If it rains, the Police Commissioner will order the Comet into the sitting room."

THE ADMINISTRATIVE LIEUTENANT MADE THE FOLLOWING ANNOUNCEMENT AT ROLL CALL:

"When it rains tomorrow at 2000 hours, the phenomenal 75 year old Chief Halley, accompanied by the Police Commissioner will drive his Comet through the station house in uniform."

AN HOUR LATER ONE OF THE COPS ASKED THE SERGEANT FOR CLARIFICATION OF THE LIEUTENANT'S ANNOUNCEMENT AT ROLL CALL AND THE SERGEANT SAID:

"Chief Halley, the new Area Commander, is going to test a new RMP here tomorrow, if it doesn't rain."

A SHORT TIME LATER, A P.A.A. ASKED THE COP IF HE KNEW WHAT WAS GOING TO HAPPEN TOMORROW, THE COP SAID:

"Forget it, you civilians can't get anything straight anyway."

Anonymous Graffiti from the NYPD

CHAPTER 1
The Two Cultures of Policing

Early in September of 1976, Francis Ianni and I, with financial support from the National Institute of Law Enforcement and Criminal Justice, began a long-term study of the social organization of the police precinct in New York City. What we learned through the two-year study, after hundreds of hours working, observing, and interviewing officers in two precincts, is that the organization of policing is best described and understood in terms of the interactions of two distinct cultures: a street cop culture and a management cop culture. These two cultures are increasingly characterized by competing and often conflicting perspectives on procedure and practice in policing. This situation is significant since much of the research and literature of policing describes the working of a monolithic single cop culture that pervades all levels of the organization. The emergence of two cultures has implications for the introduction of new techniques for management and operation, and for the introduction of new personnel policies and procedures, as well as for understanding the manner and method of the day-to-day practice of policing.

The pervasive conception of the "good old days" of policing is the organizing ethos of street cop culture, orienting individual officers and precinct social networks and defining the day-to-day job of policing. In the good old days, the public valued and respected the cop, fellow officers could be counted on and the "bosses," or higher ranking officers, were an integral part of the police family. Cops not only had public respect and the sense of security which came from belonging to a cohesive, interdependent organization, but were treated as professionals who knew their job and how best to get it done. A grateful public and an understanding city hall seldom asked how. Everybody, say the cops, knew who were the good guys and who were the bad guys, and the political system and the community they represented agreed with their definitions. Being a policeman was some-

1

thing special; a cop put his life on the line and people appreciated and respected his willingness to do so. As a result, policemen were allowed to do their jobs without too many questions or too much interference from outside the department. Not only the street cops, but everyone in the department was socialized to this ethos. Since there is no lateral entry into the department, everyone began his career as a cop and, they believed, everyone from the chief on down accepted the values of loyalty, privilege, and the importance of keeping department business inside the department. One monolithic culture permeated the department.

The police career path began with being a "good cop" who would then move to higher command positions or, in many cases, chose to remain within the same precinct, in the same assignment throughout that career. Success was based upon some combination of ability, luck, political, ethnic or family connections, or having some sponsorship in the departmental hierarchy. Even for those who made it to the top, retirement frequently meant a job (such as director of security for a corporation or hotel) where they could use their experience as a policeman to recognize the "bad guys" and use their connections in the department to take care of a situation or get information.

Because this ethos was universal throughout the department, we were told, there was one culture which everyone, whether in the street or in headquarters, shared. But a number of social and political forces have weakened that culture and as a result the organic structure of the department is disintegrating. The changing political structure of the city introduced an escalating competition for scarce resources which has had the effect of pitting agency against agency in securing jobs and fiscal allocations. Political leadership has become increasingly management-oriented as the financial excesses of the old clubhouse days very nearly bankrupted the city. For the police department as well as other city agencies, this meant greater emphasis on accountability and productivity — on management process and products that could be quantified and measured in a cost-effective equation. The new politics also included those minority groups who were disenfranchised in the old days. Ever since the civil rights movement, there has been growing political sensitivity about relationships with minority groups which holds the department accountable not only for providing adequate police service to those groups, but for affirmative action in seeking minority recruitment.

All of these forces have contributed to the development of a new headquarters management cop culture which is bureaucratically juxtaposed to the precinct street cop culture. This new management cop culture, say the cops, is positively oriented towards public administration and looks to scientific management and its associated technologies for guidance on how to run the department. Despite their new training and orientation, however, they must continue to justify their positions within the department not by their new expertise or specialization, but because at one time they were also street cops. Regulations require that they continue to display the two most important symbols of the old culture, the shield (i.e., the badge) and the gun. Unlike other bureaucratic systems, in which the upper echelon of the hierarchy is recruited from different socioeconomic and educational levels than the lower ranks, managers at all levels in the NYPD come from the same socioeconomic and work experience groups as the "workers" or cops. But, the cops maintain, their bosses have forgotten about being cops and are now professional managers. "They would give us up in a moment, if necessary, in order to save their own careers and they think we'll put up with anything because of our pension." Career paths for the managers begin when they are first assigned to headquarters, and careers in administration in the department or after retirement in business or industry are what this new breed of police administrator aspires to today.

Since our study concentrated at the precinct level of operation, we cannot explicate the values of the new management culture with the same certainty as we can with the street cop culture. However, it would seem that they are essentially those found in any managerial network in a bureaucracy and, as we shall describe through the events, are often antithetical to the values of the precinct street cop culture.

While it is improbable that any single event could transform an organization as large and complex as the New York City Police Department, many of the officers with whom we spoke during this study pointed to the Knapp Commission investigation into allegations of police corruption and its aftermath in the New York City Police Department as a kind of watershed or line of demarcation between the present reality of the policeman's job and "the good old days" of what the job used to be like.

This nostalgic sense of the good old days may or may not be an accurate interpretation of the past, but street cops believe police work should be organized and carried out that way today. The values of this culture, operationalized in maxims guiding day-to-day behavior and performance, form the reference for precinct level officers, and socialize officers to the job at the precinct. Interviews and observations of individual and collective behavior in the two precincts indicated that precinct level cops believed that a number of social and political forces have weakened the character and performance of police work and that the policing function is under strong attack as a result. According to these officers, calumny and contempt, rather than respect, are experienced daily in the community and in the media. Frequent charges of brutality and corruption have led to distrust and suspicion among policemen, and these concerns, rather than the mutuality of the old days, relates them to their bosses and the command structure. These same bosses and their political allies at city hall are tying the hands of the street cop, we were told, reducing the level of performance and making it both difficult and dangerous for police in the community. All of these forces combine to produce a new headquarters level "management cop culture," bureaucratically juxtaposed to the precinct street cop culture. What was once a family is now a factory. Now, say the street cops, not only the values, but the real loyalties of their bosses are not to the men, but to the social and political networks which embody management cop culture.

While there is some uneasy accommodation between these two cultures, they are increasingly in conflict, and this conflict isolates the precinct functionally, if not structurally, from headquarters. The isolation produces disaffection, strong stress reactions, increasing attrition of personnel, and growing problems of integrity. This in turn reinforces street cop culture resistance to attempts by headquarters managers to introduce organizational change. Instead, the precinct as a social organization rather than any loyalty to the department in general, becomes the major reference structure for the men.

Most of the officers with whom we worked see the destruction of the street cop culture as an inevitable outcome of the changing organizational character and, with obvious resignation, say that this is what the bosses want anyway because then they can more easily control cops as individuals rather than as unified groups.

The existence of these two cultures of policing is of more than academic interest. Their incongruent value systems and the differences in their expectations are major factors in the growing alienation of the street cop. This displacement of quasi-familial relationships, in which loyalties and commitments took precedence over the rule book, by the more impersonal ideology of modern management is visible in other public service sectors such as education and social welfare. Teachers and social workers, too, increasingly see their administrators as management rather than fellow professionals. Wherever this shift occurs, it produces conflict which sooner or later must affect the way a client public experiences policies and services. In many urban centers, the growing cynicism of the police is seen by citizens and supervisors alike as little different from worker disaffection in other sectors of the economy. To the street cop, at least to those I worked with, this alienation results from the inconsistencies in the variety of jobs they are expected to do; the resources they are given to do those jobs; and the compromises they must make with themselves, the public, and their jobs. Whether or not these rationalizations reflect the present relationship between the individual policeman and the structure of urban policing accurately, the critical first step in examining the disparity between policy and performance in urban policing is understanding how and why this differentiation into two cultures has occurred.

An Organizational Dilemma

The conflict of these two cultures is, in one respect, almost a classical case of what organizational theory describes as the opposition of bureaucratic and organic forms of organization. This is usually expressed as the difference between formal and informal organization. "Formal organization" refers to the formal organization chart, specifying the relations of people in the organization, while "informal organization" describes relationships or connections which are not written down or described by the formal organization chart. Management theorists often recommend beginning with the organization chart and proceeding deductively to determine patterns of informal structures in an organization (Blau, 1974). We have proceeded differently, looking at informal structures first. In doing so, we found that the formal bureaucratic structure emanating from headquarters coexisted with, rather than contained, the local precinct street culture.

From what we were told, this separation of structure was not always characteristic of the New York police department. Most of the cops I talked to believed that in the old days, the department was a cohesive organizational home for the commonly shared ethos we call street cop culture. It unified the department through a code of shared understandings and conventions of behavior binding on everyone, from the top brass to the newest recruits. The department was integrated with and accommodated to a political organization which valued them and their ethos. Because of its solidarity and integration into the political system, the department was, by and large, left to run its own affairs. The results were predictable: The mutuality and interdependence, cloaked by the secrecy which develops in such closed systems, produced both organizationally positive and socially negative results. The mutual dependence created morale and *esprit de corps*; the same mutuality and secrecy led to the institutionalization of widespread organized graft and corruption.

While the police emphasize the role of the Knapp Commission's investigations in disrupting the organic relationships this shared ethos created, other, equally important, pressures for its demise came from both inside and outside the department. Externally, a changing political system characterized by increasing attention to the rights of disenfranchised minorities and a spreading financial and social accountability led to increasing scrutiny of department management that would eventually have produced the same results. Also, as social mobility resulting from higher salaries allowed officers to purchase homes outside the city proper, social bonds were increasingly restricted to work time and were diminished in extrawork settings. The educational level of officers in the department rose along with that of the general population, but also as the result of special governmental programs intended to improve police performance through education.

Increased education made alternative job possibilities and careers outside of the department available, further reducing solidarity since one's entire career was no longer necessarily tied to the job or to relations with fellow cops. In the "good old days," the department was sexually and ethnically homogeneous; there were a few women and some minority officers, but their number and their token acceptance kept them outside the social bounds which organized the rest of the department. Pressures for minority recruitment and redress of past discrimination led to new criteria for promotional advancement, and these further eroded the sense of solidarity supported by the similarity of socioeconomic, cultural, religious and ethnic backgrounds.

Street cop culture still exists, and currently gives salience and meaning to the social organization of the precinct. But a competing ethos, concentrated at the headquarters management level, finds its salience and meaning not in the traditions of the job, but rather in theories and practices of scientific management and public administration. Management cop culture seeks to maximize the bureaucratic benefits of efficient organization, rational decision making, cost-effective procedures, and objective accountability at all levels of policing. As in all classical bureaucracies, the model proposed by management culture would do away with the organic and nonrational bounds among people as the basis for organization and decision making, substituting a consistent system of abstract rules and departmental operations and applying these rules to particular cases. It would organize departmental structure hierarchically, each lower office under the control and supervision of a higher one with authority and power distributed similarly, and would base employment and advancement on merit rather than personal characteristics or relationships. In the management model, the individual's office or role in the organizational chart (rather than personal relationships and informal networks) define what the job requires of the individual and what the individual can contribute to the organization. Since the model originated in business and industry it is not surprising that it has gradually produced a departmental structure which now, for better or worse, has a classical managers *versus* workers structure. Even more important, the two functionally defined groups have distinctive cultures which increasingly come into conflict.

Abstractly, both cultures share the goals of combating crime and insuring a safe and secure city. They differ on the definitions of these abstract concepts and, more concretely, the choice of the means by which such goals can be achieved. The street cop culture sees immediate local police response as more important than preplanned and "packaged" solutions to problems which may never occur in day-to-day police work. The street cop judges performance by the standard of "the professional cop." By "professionalism," they refer to on-the-job experience, and the experientially acquired street sense which permits them to recognize "dirty" people and situations which require police intervention. For them, this reactive "gut level" ability to recognize, identify, and respond to a situation, rather than the internalization of standardized rules and procedures, characterizes "good police work." Decision making thus takes place personally and immediately. Officers support each other, and their common interests bind them into a cohesive brotherhood. Command relationships arise in the same way and the officer's loyalty to his working peers and immediate supervisors are part of the same social bond which incorporates him and his organizational unit into larger organizational structures.

Since our study concentrated on the precinct, we did not systematically trace social networks beyond the precinct, that is, up through intervening levels to headquarters. As a result, what we know about management cop culture comes largely from what we heard and saw in the precincts as well as from a number of meetings we attended at headquarters. Those observations suggest that street cops' identification and sense of social integration seldom go beyond the precinct except where such outside forces intervene in their precinct's functioning. Management cop culture, on the other hand, concerns itself with crime on a systemwide or citywide, rather than localized, level. Management cops do care about crime at the local level, but their sense of territoriality encompasses all of the city and they must allocate resources throughout the system based upon some set of priorities. They must weigh and establish those priorities within political, social, and economic constraints and justify them within each of these contexts as well as within the policing context. Law enforcement, for the management cop, is not the immediate day-to-day interaction with a local community that the street cop sees. It is rather a carefully planned, well-designed, and efficiently implemented program in which the individual officer and the unit are impersonal resources to be used.

Our observations convinced us that precinct level or street cop culture presently determines the day-to-day practices of policing. Since the values of that culture underwrite and inform the social organization of the precinct, they determine behavior and the dispositions and attitudes of its members. I came to think of the relationship between the two cultures of policing as a form of gaming because so much of what street cops say and do emerges from their efforts to maneuver around, outwit, or nullify policy decisions from headquarters. This, however, is not meant to trivialize it, since I believe that the future character of urban policing in New York City depends on who, if anyone, wins.

The Social Organization of the Precinct and the Cop's Code

The precinct social organization can be described as a systematic set of relationships which are not nearly so informal as the characterization "informal organization" would lead one to believe. That organization is characterized by a set of emergent structures which organize social behavior and define the code of rules to which the officer is socialized. These rules are then internalized as part of the street cop culture that guides decision making and places limits on discretion and performance. While the rules emerged from observation and analyses in a policing context, I suspect that many of them are equally representative of the culturally constrained responses of people participating in any bureaucratically organized civil service culture.

While street cop culture provided the values, and thus the ends, towards which officers individually and in task groups strive, the generalized meaning of that culture must operate through some specific structures. In formal organizational analysis an organization chart describes graphically the hierarchical arrangements of roles and relationships as well as the prescribed channels of communication for information flow throughout the organization. There are no standardized graphics for presenting the informal social organization with the same degree of symbolic, if not actual, clarity. Kinship charts which look very much like organizational charts are the closest approximation but not only are they restricted in use to kinship relationships, they also tend to describe formal patterns of relationship and still cannot describe the more social interrelationships among kin.

In this model, the major functions which structure social relations in the precinct are organized into four structural domains. Each of these structures organizes a distinctive area of enculturation (learning the culture) and socialization (learning the rules of conduct) for both the formal and informal rules which guide individual and collective behavior.

The Socialization Structure

This domain organizes the system through which an officer learns from others in the precinct what the job is all about in that command. He learns what the various supervisors are like and how to work with them. He learns what is acceptable and what is not acceptable behavior. In addition to learning the values of the culture and methods for getting the job done, he is at the same time being socialized to prefer modes of behavior in the process, which is generally called "learning the system." He also learns how to evaluate his fellow officers within the definitions established by those values. He is learning, in effect, how to play the game. The traditional use of an experienced officer at the precinct, the field training specialist, as the guide to the new rookie insures the continuity of the informal rules in spite of any modernizing or "up-grading" of the curriculum.

The Authority-Power Structure

This domain organizes the authority and power of various administrative levels from headquarters and intervening levels through the chain of command into and throughout the precinct. An important element here is the difference between the power or authority derived from the legitimate position of rank and therefore the authority structure of the system, and the power which an individual may hold regardless of rank as a result of being "in the right place at the right time" or "well connected." Operationally, this means that there are several, frequently competing, authority-power systems or networks which can be called into operation in decision making, control, and accountability.

The Peer Group Structure

This domain concerns the enculturation of culturally sanctioned and socially acceptable maxims or rules for peer mediated behavior in street cop culture in general and in the specific variance of that culture found in different task groups or units within the precinct. Thus, while the values and behaviors particular to street cop culture are shared to some extent by all police officers (including many management cops), they differ among and between ranks or subunits.

Cross-Group Structures

This domain includes the enculturation of behavior codes for interaction between the precinct and other departmental levels which includes definitions of mediator roles and communication styles (including the importance of the grapevine as an information collection and dissemination network). Socialization within this area defines how supervisors relate to the men and how the men, in turn, relate to several levels of supervisory authority, as well as the relative rights and responsibilities of each. A very important control dimension involves the role of sergeant as a firstline supervisor. Of considerable importance, but often ignored, is the process of mediation between the two networks. Mediator roles can be quite formal, as in the case of the Patrolmen's Benevolent Association (PBA) representatives and officials, personnel officers, or official departmental grievance channels. Many unformalized roles, however, emerge in the pattern of relationships established in the precinct. The "rabbi" or "hook" (commonly used expressions referring to individuals with connections), for example, can connect a high ranking officer at headquarters with a street cop because the two might have been partners at one time in their careers. Critical here is the system of exchange of favors, and "owing" someone for a previous favor, which can be "called in" at any time.

While these structures organize or contain varieties of social action, they are most visible in the major processes by which the four structures are operationalized in the social organization of the day-to-day life of the precinct and which adjust the structures to changing demographic, political, social, and economic conditions. These processes appeared with such regularity and persistence in the research that we believe them to be basic for organizing social interaction within and across each of the four major structures in the precinct.

The process of *sorting*, in which individuals classify themselves and each other according to a set of culturally defined labels (which may differ somewhat from precinct to precinct), is fundamental in defining the patterns of social relationships and work relationships. Police officers sort each other and they are sorted by supervisors and other administrators. The discrepancy between the sorting carried out in street cop culture and that which is part of management cop culture is at the heart of some of the tensions and conflicts between these two cultures. The street cop who takes care of his own business on department time may be viewed as getting back at the system by his precinct peers, but he is in violation of department rules and regulations according to management. Similarly, the precinct commanding officer who informally accepts such behavior from men who otherwise "deliver when there is a job to be done," may be considered a "good boss" by his men, but a poor supervisor by his superiors. Changes in the sorting process over time usually indicate positive or negative interpretations of the authority-power, peer group, or cross-group structures, because they modify the pattern of social contact within a particular precinct. In organizational terms sorting establishes for each officer categories of "generalized others," based on what can be expected from them and how they will interact in a given situation. Thus, a cop can depend on an officer in the same squad under most circumstances, usually more than an officer from another precinct, and he can depend on officers in general more than on a boss or a civilian.

The process of *territoriality* includes the formal and informal relationship between environment and behavior within the precinct and between the precinct and other environments. There are obvious relationships between space and behavior within the precinct such as those observable in the locker room, around the station house desk, or in the radio car. Similarly, as in the contrast between the Bronx and Manhattan precincts, the characteristics of a precinct community may distinguish a range of individual and collective behaviors. What is more important, however, is what we know about the relationship between organizational behavior and environment. Organizations are affected by their environment in many ways, but possibly most importantly in the characteristic way in which effective decision making depends on the level in the organization at which the decisions are made. The most effective level is dependent on the fit between the environment and the decision to be made. This suggests that in diverse and rapidly changing environments, a condition which characterizes discretionary and reactive occupational cultures such as policing, it is necessary for many decisions to be made at relatively low administrative or command levels because of the need for immediate response. Different kinds of decisions are appropriate to different levels. Policy decisions involving police organization and control, for example, need to be made fairly high up. In day-to-day policework, however, responsiveness to the immediate territorial and behavioral environment and situation is more crucial, demanding more flexible parameters, and so decisions are more appropriately made at lower levels. In such cases, the relative importance of each decision — that is, its potential "organizational cost" — is assumed to be much less.

Within the department and even within the precinct, territoriality may also be seen to affect the attitudes and actions of different subunits within the organization. Thus, subunit specialization may be required to deal with the varying demands and requirements of the organization's environment. This same specialization, however, means that each unit and level will have a different approach to issues that arise. It is important to keep in mind that this is not only a matter of subgroup loyalties, although these are important as was pointed out earlier. It is also a matter of the kind of environment which the different subunits are in the habit of responding to and the information which they have about the dependence of their portion of the organization on the whole.

Applying these concepts of organization and environment to the distinctions we have pointed out between street cop culture and management cop culture adds some further details to the factors which underwrite the problem of departmental organization. There are a number of pragmatic and historical reasons for the many conflicts between the two cultures. Under the old system idealized in street cop culture, precinct policing was a localized and relatively autonomous process with a precinct commander in charge. The precinct dealt with the local people and, as long as there were no major disturbances which attracted attention to it, they were left pretty much to themselves. Certainly they had obligations to headquarters and presumably through headquarters to the political system, but generally, they were well integrated into their territory. Since there was much less mobility from precinct to precinct, this sense of ownership of "turf" increased over time. Under the new system, the management cop culture centralized much of the decision making power of the department and consequently, at least in the view of the street cop, took away much of the discretionary decision making power at the interface between the precinct and its community. In addition, they increased the number of activities for which both the individual officer and the precinct were responsible through the establishment of standardized reporting and accountability systems. Under the assumption that familiarity breeds corruption, assignment of commanding officers to precincts were frequently changed and men were also transferred with greater frequency. The new management cop culture thus represents a loss of local autonomy because it imposes tighter external supervision over more areas of activity.

The process of *rule making and rule breaking* serves as another means of organizing behavior within and among the four major structures. In the precinct there is a continual proliferation of rules and procedures. There is also, however, differential enforcement of rules. The differences may lie across categories (such as between supervisors and men, or between individual enforcers and offenders), over time, or in different places. All of the component factors which cause rules to be made in particular situations and to be variously enforced depending on personnel or circumstances, provide indicators of the social organization of the precinct.

Collectively, these processes which mold and channel behavior within the previously identified four structures are expressed in the form of behavioral expectations and conventions which set the limits for approved behavior in the precinct. We have come to call this loose collection of understandings the "cop's code." This code describes a charter for action, a set of shared understandings which, while not written down or formalized, are understood by all members of the precinct and limit the degrees of variability of behavior permissible for individuals. Such limitations are the price one pays for group membership. It is the charter which provides the formal component in what is usually considered the informal system of social organization in the precinct. A senior officer, for example, will allow certain degrees of freedom for a more junior partner's behavior either in the socialization structure, in the authority-power structure or, in some cases, in both. Similarly, a supervisor will allow variability in a police officer's behavior until the variation exceeds the limits established by the code's definition of officer behavior, before he invokes the code's sanctions. Invocation is also used frequently by a lower person or group to a higher person or group as a means of redressing some perceived wrong which exceeds the limits established by the code. This is often the case in relations between a sergeant and the men he is supervising.

Our research experience confirms the cops' belief that supervisors are usually reluctant to make decisions or absolute rules which might set a fixed pattern of enforcement. This reluctance to impose specific rules means that much of the "family" life of the precinct proceeds from the shared understanding of the code rather than from such specific rules. The process of invocation of the code comes to represent the major social control mechanism within the precinct.

Violating one of these rules, which reach through the peer group and socialization structure into the street cop culture, will mean social criticism and sanctions because "you're not behaving like one of us." It not only shapes their behavior but also distinguishes or sorts the "good" cop from the "bad" cop. In the sense that we use it here, controls within this social system begin with shared values and expectations that ultimately become internalized as maxims which carry with them sets of sanctions when they are not followed. We extracted a set of maxims or injunctions from our observations and interviewing in both precincts which have such a code. Once we had developed our version of the cop's code, we read them back to cops in both precincts and elsewhere in the department to see if our list was recognizable to them. In this process we discovered that there are really two sets of maxims which make up the cop's code. One regulates relationships in the peer group and relates street cops to each other. The other set of maxims, which we believe is becoming increasingly powerful and pertinent as a result of the tension between the two cultures, relates street cops to bosses.

A number of researchers and writers have described specific aspects of the cop's informal code of conduct. Westley (1953), for example, notes that the code forbids police from informing against fellow officers. This code of secrecy is also described by Stoddard (1968), Westley (1956), and Savitz (1971). Skolnick (1966) suggests that danger, and the authority that officers may exert against civilians, contributes to a sense of solidarity which makes them isolated and dependent on each other. This interdependence provides the basis for a code which is characterized by suspiciousness, clannishness and secrecy: Rubinstein (1973) presents a number of maxims which he saw in operation in Philadelphia. These center around aspects of the cop's job. Thus, in exercising authority, the cop learns to assess the physical control of the situation, he learns how to "bullshit" to avoid using force. A good cop always wins and must learn to control his fears by looking for signs of danger, and learn the quickness, resolution and decisiveness which will urge him forward when others withdraw. He must show courage in the face of danger or potential danger, and a distinction is made between a cop who is *willing* to use force and one who is *eager* to use force. An officer either unwilling to use force, or overeager, is viewed as a danger to everyone who works with him. Manning (1977) points out that because of discretion, the code is made up of rules which are usually site-specific. He sees a general cynicism about rules which come from above and sees the "cover you ass" response as particularly important.

The Cop's Code

The cop's code, which responds to street cop culture in defining relationships with other cops, contains the following maxims:

Watch out for you partner first and then the rest of the guys working that tour. This rule is fundamental and expresses both the strong sense of dependency and mutuality and the sorting that takes place among peers. "Watching out" means looking out for the interests as well as the physical safety of the other guy.

Don't give up another cop. This is an injunction to secrecy which is based on social bonding and might better conclude "and he won't give *you* up." Here again we see the importance of sorting since there are situations in which, as in the case of Officer Kelly and the officer who committed suicide, being a cop does not necessarily mean being "one of us."

Show balls. This enjoins the individual to be a man and not to back down, particularly in front of civilians: Once you've got yourself into a situation, take control and see it through.

Be aggressive when you have to, but don't be too eager. This is related to the previous maxim but has a somewhat different connotation. Old timers will tell new men that when a situation develops, get on it but don't be too eager and go looking for trouble. If you get a radio run (i.e., a call) on a crime in progress, for example, it will probably end up being a "past" crime, or unfounded, by the time you get there anyway, so don't break your neck getting there.

Don't get involved in anything in another guy's sector. This outgrowth of territoriality means that you should not interfere in another man's work space because he is accountable and must live with the consequences. In the old days, we are told, this was phrased, "Don't muscle in on someone else's action on his turf."

Hold up your end of the work. Here the cop is told that if he slacks off unreasonably or too frequently, somebody else has to take up that slack.

If you get caught off base, don't implicate anybody else. This is an extension of both the "Don't give up another cop" and "Show balls" maxims. Getting caught off base, which can range from being out of your sector to more serious or illegal activities, is likely to bring trouble or attention to the entire group. Anyone who is caught should take his punishment and not implicate others.

Make sure the other guys know if another cop is dangerous or "crazy." This means that while you would not give such a person up to the bosses, you should let other cops, who might be working with and depending on him, know what to expect.

Don't trust a new guy until you have checked him out. Because the social bonds are so strong and because of the increasing suspicion about field associates, it is necessary to use the grapevine to find out the previous history of any newcomer to the precinct.

Don't tell anybody else more than they have to know, it could be bad for you and it could be bad for them. Generally this means not to volunteer information because you may involve someone else when they don't want to be.

Don't talk too much or too little. Both are suspicious. What this means is that following the norm is important. Someone who talks too much is known as a "big mouth" and may be covering up, and someone who talks too little may be afraid to say too much about himself.

Don't leave work for the next tour. This covers a number of possibilities: leaving the car without gas or not taking a complaint report or anything that means the next tour has to clean up after you.

There are other less persuasive maxims such as "Always take the same vacation days as your partner" since if you don't, he might get stuck working with someone who is probably available only because no one else wants to work with him. There are also specific job or situation maxims as well, but those listed above were found in both precincts and were recognized by everyone with whom we spoke.

The cop's code also contains maxims concerning relationships with the management cop culture through the authority-power structure:

Protect your ass. An implicit assumption here is, "If the system wants to get you, it will," and so the prudent officer makes certain that he is covered. This injunction is indicative of the increasing individualism and isolation felt by street cops but the attitude and its behavioral consequences are just as pervasive among headquarters cops. Traditionally, we are told, when one culture unified the department, the system protected the individual; now it is every man for himself.

Don't make waves. Here again the maxim advises that the officer not be a "troublemaker" in the bosses' eyes but it also says "Don't mess with the system." Being a troublemaker means that supervisors pay more attention to you, and consequently you bring unnecessary attention to what your peers might be doing as well. Asking too many questions about procedures or making too many suggestions about how the system might be improved also brings too much attention from the bosses.

Don't give them too much activity. If you are "too eager" and increase your productivity in a given month, says this maxim, you bring unnecessary pressure and attention not only to yourself but to your peers as well. Next month "they" will expect you to do even better than you did this month and they will also question why your peers are not giving them as much work as you are. In the old days, increased productivity could mean favorable attention which might lead to a detective's shield or at least a few days off from your commanding officer (CO). Now, because of the financial crisis, there is little possibility of advancement anyway.

Keep out of the way of any boss from outside your precinct. In the day-to-day life and work of the precinct, the officer comes to an accommodation with the precinct bosses in terms of what they expect and what they will tolerate and so he knows the limits placed on his behavior. Any boss from outside the precinct is an unknown authority figure who might report a cop to a command level outside the precinct. This transfers control from the organic relationships within the precinct to the unknown and impersonal control of the departmental authority structure and its formal rules and procedures.

Don't look for favors just for yourself. Here again, the solidarity of street cop culture tells the officer to look out for his peers in relating to the bosses. This is most frequently expressed in terms of not "sucking up to the old man" (the CO) or to the administrative lieutenant who, in their roles, deal more with the officer as an individual than as a member of a work group. The lieutenant and patrol sergeants on your tour, however, are directly related to ongoing work conditions and keeping them happy will hopefully keep them "off everybody's back" during that tour.

Don't take on the patrol sergeant by yourself. Since the patrol sergeant is in direct supervisory control of the officer and his peers in the task group, the immediacy of the relationship means that his working relationship with the men sets the tone for that tour. Applying pressure against a patrol sergeant in retaliation for a real or perceived wrong will work only if all your peers cooperate.

Know your bosses. One of the first questions an officer asks when he "turns out" is, "Who's working and who has the desk?" He is questioning what bosses are around on that tour and specifically who has final say on that tour. Knowing the bosses means that you can adjust your expectations and activities for the tour to what you know about *their* expectations and style of supervision.

Don't do the bosses' work for them. In operational terms this means that if an officer knows that a peer is shirking his duty or involved in misconduct, it is not his responsibility to tell a boss about it. While the sense of mutual protection is one source for this attitude, it is sometimes expressed as, "The boss gets paid for doing that."

Don't trust bosses to look out for your interest. This maxim represents the street cop's view of life at the top. The management cop, it is supposed, finds it just as necessary or expedient to "protect his ass" from his superiors as the street cop does. If he has to choose between you and himself, "He's going to make the same decision you would." A number of officers attributed this to the fact that once the officer "climbs up the ladder he holds on for dear life," particularly at appointive ranks above captain.

CHAPTER 2

Police Work

Major urban police departments are experiencing increasing pressures for change and responsiveness to such public concerns as demands for better educated personnel who come from a variety of racial and ethnic backgrounds. Such personnel bring new life-patterns and values into police work. At the same time, such issues as the increased use of female police officers at all levels of police work, and greater civilian and community involvement, promise to produce even greater demands for changes in police organization. These demands arise within an occupational climate of increasing concern over job security and job satisfaction, corruption and ethics, and rapid social and technological change. These issues combine to produce major questions concerning organizational patterns designed to maximize efficient and effective police work. Despite considerable research showing that more socialization, and thus more influence on operational decision making, takes place in the peer-mediated social systems of the precinct and its subunits, we know little about how those systems interact with the formal organization of the police department or how they might be used to enhance police responsiveness to changing conditions. Because management cop culture has developed out of modern management theory and thus views police organizations as analogous to those in government and business, most urban police administrators have ignored the issue, as well as the relevant research on the social organization of the police.

The analogy with business and government suggests that departments resemble businesses and governments, but tells us virtually nothing about how their organization facilitates the police officer's day-to-day contacts with citizens, peers, and supervisors; nor does it describe the organization in relation to the values and goals which make policing unique and distinct. As a result, we know little about how urban policing units might be organized for more effective job performance or how the many facilitative, extraorganizational "learning" systems through which police learn "on-the-job," intersect with the organization of urban police departments.[1] Yet we need only look at current trends in policing — increasing emphasis on a service model, demand for improved community relations and citizen involvement, human relations and ethical awareness workshops, and decentralization of authority and control — to realize that police administrators now sense that the informal social systems that operate in every precinct or police unit may also be among the primary facilitators of effective policing. Many administrators, however, continue to propose new human relations approaches, integrity programs, and personnel or career path structures in a conceptual vacuum. Specifically, they have a "gut feeling" that informal social systems in the precinct are important, but have no clear understanding of what makes the informal social networks so critical to policing, nor how they operate. As administrators attempt to develop new programs aimed at reducing the discrepancy between "downtown" and the police officer's precinct subculture, they seem compelled to somehow force these new programs into the existing formal structure of the department. That structure eventually corrupts the function, frustrates the administrator and usually increases the officers' alienation and cynicism.

Policing, at every level, depends on decision making. Management needs to make decisions and needs the power to do so. Whether the issue is recruiting minority personnel or handling family disputes, it presents police administrators and patrol officers with decision making situations. Experts may disagree on which approach is best suited to problem solving, but all agree that problem identification and some means of information gathering are essential.

Administrators have tried a variety of approaches to problem identification and information seeking. At one time or another, authoritarian, intuitive, rational, empirical, pragmatic, and consensual modes have been tried, individually and collectively; each has its adherents. Reduced to its essentials, however, the conflict over how best to identify organizational or managerial problems and to seek data necessary for problem solving and decision making embodies a tension between those who look to the folklore of the job and those who seek scientific or rational solutions to management problems.

Each method may be valid, but each also has its limitations. The experiential empiricism of conventional folk-wisdom or "war stories" of practice provide an existential mode of problem identification, at least of the practical problems of day-to-day policing. It does not, however, provide a means of systematic data seeking or of generalizing beyond individual experience, and is consequently easily dismissed by those looking for scientific solutions. Many established police procedures and practices thereby escape serious questioning or attention. Routine data collected, including activity logs, arrest and crime coding sheets, and statistics on response time, provide standardized means of gathering information on the job. But field personnel frequently dismiss the data and the findings derived from them as irrelevant to their problems. As a result, many practitioners fail to use any research-generated data for improving practice or setting policy. Social science research on policing over the last few decades has given us considerable information relevant to police, even if much of it merely points to what does not work and some suggestions as to why not.

The Occupational Culture

A pervasive myth, encouraged by the mass media (and the police themselves), is that the police spend the majority of their time investigating crimes. In fact, the police spend most of their time resolving conflicts, maintaining and restoring order, and providing social services:

> They rush accident victims to the hospital; bring alcoholics indoors on a winter's night; break into a locked house or apartment to see whether an elderly occupant is alive and well; persuade a mentally ill person who has barricaded himself in his apartment to return to the hospital; administer emergency first aid to a heart attack victim while waiting for the ambulance to come. Police also get cats down from trees, chauffeur dignitaries around town, rescue the drowning, talk suicidal people out of killing themselves, direct traffic, and provide advice and help to the sick and elderly, as well as to otherwise healthy people who simply cannot cope with some pressing problem (Silberman, 1978, p. 203).

Although part of a semimilitary, bureaucratic organization, the patrolman exercises wide discretion in carrying out these functions. Who to stop? Who to arrest? How to obtain and record information? How to settle a family dispute? Detailed police manuals or patrol guides do not answer these questions. This emphasis on discretion (Bittner, 1967; Black, 1968; Westley, 1953) has led a number of researchers (Wilson, 1974; Silberman, 1978) to emphasize the artistry of police work: the complexity of the job, the ambiguity of choices, the necessity for wisdom. Results range from great successes to great blunders. The ideal patrolman should be a "philosopher-king" and have a "tragic vision of life" (Muir, 1977). Others find a patrolman's job considerably more prosaic:

> They do engage in chases, in gunfights, in careful sleuthing. But these are rare events. Most police work resembles any other kind of work: it is boring, tiresome, sometimes dirty, sometimes technically demanding, but it is rarely dangerous (Manning, 1977, p. 134).

While there is some evidence that mining, agriculture, and construction are more dangerous than police work there is considerable literature that suggests the constant threat of danger is unique to policing and is anxiety producing. Other researchers suggest that it is the system itself that creates the anxiety (Denyer, Callender, and Thompson, 1975). The cop is a clerk in a squad car unable to follow up cases and getting no credit for helping solve crimes. He is frustrated by the courts and by vice laws that no one believes in but which he must enforce. He recycles the same drunks and juveniles. Becoming trapped in police routine, he aspires to "day work" or detective work. His circle of civilian friends shrinks and his marriage is strained.

There is a debate, then, as to how demanding, exciting, and rewarding police work is. There is also a debate as to how demanding, exciting and rewarding police work could be. Could it and should it become a profession? Or is just a job? What kind of training or education makes the best policeman?

Police work has other dilemmas. There is apparent almost immediately the dilemma of choosing between the professional ideal of policing learned at the academy and the experiential pragmatism encountered at the precinct. The new recruit is indoctrinated in a "get tough" ideology. Starting at the bottom as a foot patrolman, he must learn new jargon and rituals. He must quickly learn that one of the important arts he must master is the sense of when to take action and when not to take action. An officer who brings too many cases into the station is considered incompetent, an officer who brings in too few is considered a shirker (Niederhoffer, 1967). What is consistent about policing is its uncertainty. Policing is said to be reactive and while some officers claim such unpredictability of the job is exciting, others point to the stress it produces.

There is also a good deal of speculation on the modal police personality, typical values, and political beliefs. "The policeman's culture is that of the masculine working man. It is of the docks, the barracks, the battle-fields. . . ." Politically, the policeman is "a conservative, perhaps reactionary person of lower class or lower middle class origin, often a supporter of radical right causes, often prejudiced and repressive, often extremely ambivalent about the rights of others" (Skolnick, 1966, p. 82).

Cynicism comes easily, skepticism is required, and disillusionment comes early. "An officer may begin his career by accepting as truth whatever he is told, but his experiences quickly encourage caution" (Rubinstein, 1973, p. 233). A veteran cop sums up his experience with policing:

> The whole job is a joke, you start out with delusions of grandeur — how you're gonna save the world. But you find out soon enough that nobody cares. The people in the suburbs don't care as long as you keep it confined to the city, and the judges don't care as long as their dockets are current (Silberman, 1978, p. 240).

Other personality characteristics have been suggested. One of the first things that the new officer does is to promptly lose his nonpolice friends. He learns that only other officers can understand him and that he must stick with the group. He tends to be hypersensitive to criticism, especially from outsiders. Personal isolationism, group coalescence, and defensiveness lead to secretiveness (Stoddard, 1968; Savitz, 1971; Reiss, 1968), suspicion (Hahn, 1971; Skolnick, 1966), and occupational solidarity (Westley, 1953; Skolnick, 1966) and the debate is over whether these are functional to policing, and if so, how much so. There is contradictory research evidence that the policeman is both more authoritarian (Mc-Namara, 1967) and less authoritarian (Bayley and Mendelsohn, 1969) than the average citizen.

Cynical, authoritarian, conforming, prejudiced, lower middle class, often brutal — the picture offered in both the popular press and social research is not always attractive. Yet anyone hazarding generalizations about the personalities of 400,000 American policemen is bound to be challenged on grounds of inconclusive evidence. A major survey of the extensive literature on police personality concluded:

> We began with the assumption that policemen are very unusual people, set apart from the rest of the population by virtue of their authoritarian mentality. Now it looks like policemen may be rather ordinary people, not greatly unlike other Middle-Americans. We cannot even be sure there is such a thing as a police personality, however loosely we define it (More, 1976, p. 125).

It is not surprising, then, that there is a continuing debate as to whether the job creates the type of officer or whether certain types are attracted to the job.

Police administrators, as well as social and behavioral scientists, want to know what kind of person makes the best policeman. Once such information is available, they reason, personnel procedures can be developed which will not only encourage such people to become policemen, but will enable them to weed out much earlier those applicants and recruits who might eventually create problems for the department.

Organization of the New York City Police Department (NYPD)

Like most police departments throughout the world, the NYPD has a paramilitary structure. Police administrators usually explain this by the functional similarity to military organizations — both involving a uniformed force bearing arms and requiring a strict emphasis on discipline, and command distinction based on a hierarchy of ranks, in order to insure task performance. The number of ranks in any police department is generally a function of size. The vast majority of departments throughout the country, in small suburban or rural areas, consist of a chief and perhaps seven or eight men. In larger departments, the military command structure that increases authority and rank from sergeant to lieutenant to captain and up, is most common. Unlike the military, however, once the police officer moves from patrolman to sergeant, he has made the transition to a "boss." Since there is no lateral entry into police work, everyone starts as a patrolman and there is no officer caste as in the military.

In New York City, promotion up to and including captain is achieved through a competitive civil service examination given periodically by the department. Promotions above captain are appointed by the police commissioner (PC) and continue at his (or his successor's) pleasure. There is a structured line of promotion upward by appointment from captain to deputy inspector to inspector to deputy chief to assistant chief and from there to the three-star "super chiefs" who command the five major bureaus (field services, detectives, organized crime control, personnel, and inspectional services) and the four-star chief of operations (the highest uniformed rank). It is possible for the commissioner to jump someone up one or more ranks in these appointed grades (colloquially referred to as "captain with friends"). An officer may be removed from any of these appointed ranks by the police commissioner, but would retain his highest civil service rank of captain.

The New York City Charter places all power in the position of police commissioner. However, practice demands some degree of decentralization of authority which is as variable as the dictates of command, leadership style, city hall, or community pressure at the time. The structure and organization of power and authority is not as neat as an organizational chart of the NYPD would have one believe. Perhaps the department is most like the classical civil service bureaucracy in the way "reform" commissioners, "progressive" commissioners, "conservative" commissioners and even civilian commissioners come and go, but, say department sages, operationally nothing much changes.

The police commissioner (PC) is the head of the department and is appointed by the mayor for a term of five years. Directly beneath the PC are seven deputy commissioners: the first deputy commissioner, who is acting head of the department in the PC's absence, and the deputy commissioners for administration, community affairs, trials, public information, criminal justice, and legal matters. While the deputy commissioners are "civilian" positions, the commissioner and the first deputy are usually police officers who have come up through the ranks. The PC, the deputies, the chief of operations, the bureau chiefs, and their staffs (approximately 4400 sworn members of the force) comprise headquarters, which is located in the lower downtown area, close to city hall and the mayor's office. It is variously referred to as "downtown," "headquarters," or by its official address, 1 Police Plaza.

The field units of the department, which report through the chief of field services, are organized by geographical location in the five boroughs of New York City. The borough, or area, command level is responsible for maintaining police services for an entire borough and is in direct line of command over the constituent precincts in its geographical area.

Because of size, the boroughs of Manhattan and Brooklyn have two borough (or area) commands, one each for the north and south area precincts in those boroughs. The commander of a borough is usually an assistant chief, but occasionally someone with the rank of inspector or deputy chief may function in that capacity on a temporary basis. The borough office, located in one of its precinct station houses, is administratively subdivided into several sections including specialized units which are responsible for the entire borough. Some inspectors have administrative control over groups of precincts (usually two or three) within an area or borough command. All precinct paper work (i.e., crime and personnel activity statistics and reports) are channeled through the borough to headquarters units. Similarly, directives from headquarters units are passed down through the borough level to the precinct. There is a great variability of style among borough chiefs and job folklore suggests that a precinct commander's life is made easier or harder by the character or style of the borough commander, while the life of the officer on patrol is little affected.

New York City and its five boroughs are divided into 73 patrol precincts responsible for police service and protection of approximately 319.8 square miles and approximately eight million people. Police work is the responsibility of approximately 25,000 men and women, most of whom are assigned to the field service bureau which coordinates police patrol throughout the city, twenty-four hours a day, seven days a week. Additional officers work in specialized, citywide units including traffic, special operations, detective bureau, organized crime control, and inspectional services.

The city's 73 precincts are administered from station houses which are the direct service-delivery field commands to which most policemen and policewomen are assigned. The precinct encompasses an area which is subdivided into geographically defined radio patrol car sectors with a letter designation (sectors Adam, Boy, Charlie, etc.), which are then further divided into smaller foot and scooter patrol posts. The number and size of the sectors are based upon the number of radio cars assigned to that precinct, which corresponds to the percentage of crimes and calls for service in that precinct.

Radio cars patrol with two officers[3] who constitute a team, referred to as "partners" or "steady partners,"[4] if they work together on a regular basis.

Assignment to foot patrol means the officer patrols by walking an area extending for several blocks along a major avenue or business street.

One officer quite aptly summed up the differences among precincts in New York City: "Precincts are like women, essentially they're all the same. Some of the external goodies might make one more attractive than the other . . . they're all alike."

Precinct operations occur at the direct interface with the surrounding community. Precinct administrative staff and the officers on foot, in radio cars, in unmarked cars or on scooters who patrol the precinct are the visible representation of law enforcement to the citizens of New York City. Within the precinct, personnel are divided in several different ways: formally, by function and rank hierarchy as represented by the organization chart; and informally by affiliation, experience, and such shared characteristics as sex, ethnicity, and religion.

The precinct operates twenty-four hours a day, seven days a week, with no holidays. Officers work an eight-hour day, broken into three segments, or tours of duty, from 8 a.m. to 4 p.m. (the "day tour" or 8x4), 4 p.m. to 12 p.m. (4x12), and 12 p.m. to 8 a.m. (12x8 or the "late tour"). The precinct is a self-sustaining unit of operation under the command of the precinct commanding officer (CO) who usually holds the rank of captain. Recently there has been talk of returning to a previous system where deputy inspectors commanded certain high activity precincts. Precincts are classified by headquarters as high, medium, or low activity, according to such characteristics as the number of complaints handled by the precinct, the type of crime activity, and the presence of certain groups such as very vocal minorities, political activists, or highly influential citizens.

Personnel allocations are based on an equation including the number of calls for service in that precinct, number of crimes reported, and any unusual conditions in the area. The precinct's primary policing responsibility is to the geographical community it serves and manpower is deployed according to the commanding officer's judgment of community crime and crime prevention priorities. Occasionally precinct personnel will be pulled out of the precinct and sent to special citywide details, such as parades, riots, strikes, special events such as the Democratic National Convention, or the protection of prominent visitors to the city.

While the number of police officers in a precinct varies with its size and activity level, most NYPD precincts contain about 200–250 officers. The precinct CO relies on two levels of supervision between himself and the patrol force. Direct supervision is the responsibility of the lieutenants and sergeants assigned to that precinct. Immediately below the CO is the executive captain. While not responsible for setting command policy, he assumes command for an eight-hour period when the CO is off duty. The "exec" will usually work a 4x12 when the CO works an 8x4 tour.

Officers are assigned to a squad of six to eight men that work according to a "chart" or duty schedule. Each squad works a certain tour for four or five consecutive days, then gets two days off and comes back to work another tour. Thus, an officer might work four days of 8x4's, take two days off, come back to work four days of 4x12's, take his days off, and come back to five days of 12x8's. Over the years, the issue of such working hours and having to adjust physically, mentally, and socially to working days and nights has been blamed by officers and their union leaders for causing low morale, illness, stress symptoms, and marital problems.

Patrol sergeants are responsible for the supervision of several squads of officers on a day-to-day basis, and they in turn are responsible to the several lieutenants assigned to the precinct.

A precinct station house is the police equivalent of a military outpost or field unit, but it is also a unit in the bureaucracy and, in keeping with the nature of bureaucracy, there is increasingly more paper work. This requires a precinct office staff ("the palace guard" as they are referred to more or less affectionately by patrol officers) responsible for preparing and forwarding all reports and communications between the precinct and other administrative levels. These staff positions are under the direct supervision of the administrative lieutenant (sometimes a sergeant) who reports directly to the CO. Included in the precinct staff are roll call officers responsible for assignment of officers to various duties such as radio, foot, or scooter patrol, as well as seeing to it that officers are informed of court appearances; the time-records man, responsible for recording time worked, overtime, sick time, etc.; and the planning and statistical officer, who keeps the precinct's activity records for arrests and summons, and follows patterns of crime activity in the area. Civilian employees are frequently assigned to work as clerical assistants to these staff positions. Specialists such as highway safety, crime prevention, warrants, and community relations officers also work out of the precinct station house.

While most officers are assigned to a sector car or foot post, specialized patrol activity is conducted by units such as anticrime and "conditions" teams. These officers work out of uniform and patrol in unmarked cars looking for specific street crimes or certain local illegal or disruptive conditions (such as prostitution or burglaries) which the CO has decided need special attention. These officers do not handle the usual calls coming from the central dispatch, which are the responsibility of the regular sector cars. A radio car team is normally assigned one sector; however, depending on the number of cars available on that tour, the team might have the added responsibility of one or two additional sectors.

At any time of day or night the precinct will have five or six radio cars patroling the community streets plus several unmarked cars with anticrime officers. In addition, a conditions unit might be "sitting" on a location watching for drug sales, burglaries or prostitutes. During any tour there will also be a patrol sergeant assigned to supervise the men as they respond to radio runs or walk foot posts, noting the officers' response time (the amount of time it takes from when the call is dispatched to a radio car to when the officer calls back to the dispatcher indicating that the call has been taken care of) and verifying their presence on post. The type of "job" or call given out by the central dispatcher to the officers in a patrol car is coded to a number designation and responses or dispositions are similarly numerically coded. In some cases (such as a bomb threat, or an occurrence in a licensed premise) a radio car is not allowed to respond without a supervisor or higher ranking officer present. Officers are assigned meal breaks before they leave the station house ("turn out") to take their assigned post. Meals are staggered so that there is always a radio patrol car on the street. Strict regulations, such as not being able to leave precinct boundaries, cover the taking of meal breaks.

When the police officer arrives at the station house, he usually goes directly to his locker and changes into his uniform. The officers working that particular tour then gather in the muster room for roll call, assignments, information on some current situation affecting the command, and occasionally some words of praise or caution from the CO. Sometimes, depending on the attitude of the CO toward inspection, the officers will be inspected for proper uniform, personal appearance, proper equipment, etc., and then will be turned out to begin their tour of duty. Most precincts turn out some cars on the half hour and others on the hour to insure continual street coverage. Otherwise all of the officers from the previous tour would be off the streets a few moments before the end of the tour, and the outgoing platoon would not be out on the streets until several moments after the hour. At the start of every tour each officer begins a new activity log for the day in his memo book, a leather-bound book which he must carry at all times. In this book he records the complete activity of that tour including assignments received, activities performed, absences from post, and the time of completion of his tour. This record is critical in recalling occurrences at a later date for court appearances, departmental complaints, etc. At some time during the tour, the sergeant on patrol will initial one of the pages which indicates that the officer was seen on the street performing his job.

Because of the presence of large numbers of officers working out of uniform in street crime units not necessarily assigned to the precinct in which they are currently working and therefore unfamiliar to the precinct officers, it was necessary to devise some identifying symbol for safety in responding to radio runs. For this reason a citywide "color of the day" is selected and is exhibited as a headband varying in color from day to day. This color designation is also used when calling other departmental offices to identify the caller as someone in the department or "on the job."

The desk lieutenant (lieutenants are usually called "Lou," and sergeants "Sarge") is the officer responsible for the precinct during the tour that he is working. Thus, while the precinct commanding officer has command responsibility for the precinct twenty-four hours a day (even when he is not at the precinct), the desk lieutenant, who sits behind the station house desk on the main floor, is operationally responsible for all precinct activity during his tour of duty. While the officers working any particular tour are usually assigned by the roll call officer to the same radio car, partner, foot or scooter posts, unusual conditions at the beginning or during the tour might necessitate a change in their regular assignment. Such decisions are the responsibility of the desk lieutenant, as well as maintaining the precinct record on individuals arrested, stolen property recovered or released, and signing off on any reports prepared by the complaint room or by officers during their tour. He is also responsible for the conduct of all officers working that eight-hour tour.

The use of civilians for certain jobs in the department is not new, but increased financial restrictions and a freeze on hiring of new officers have necessitated a very controversial push to "civilianize" many jobs traditionally held by police officers. Usually civilians can be found working in the 124 (complaint) room, manning the telephone switchboard (TS) and otherwise assisting precinct staff officers.

One of the most significant changes in policing has been the notion of the police specialist and specialty squads, but to date the patrol precinct is still the most basic unit of policing and the patrol officer still the final link in whatever process begins with management policies and directives and ends with two officers riding through the street in a radio car. Although the police commissioner has ultimate authority over the department, and superior officers have various levels or degrees of authority dependent on their rank, function, and position in the hierarchy, the uniformed police officer is the most visible symbol of the department and consequently must, whether he aspires to or not, symbolize the authority, effectiveness, and ultimately the morality and integrity of the entire department.

Notes

1. For some excellent exceptions, see Van Maanen (1972), Skolnick (1966), Rubinstein (1973), Westley (1970), and Niederhoffer (1967).
2. See also McNamara (1967), Wilson (1968), Bittner (1970), and the President's Commission on Law Enforcement and the Administration of Justice (1969).
3. Towards the conclusion of our study, a new program was introduced as an economy measure with one man or "solo" cars patrolling certain precincts and/or certain sectors.
4. For more detail on the significance of radio car partners in policing, see Radano (1968) and Walker (1969).

CHAPTER 3

The Precinct Communities

We were interested in precinct-level behavior but knew, through prior experience with the New York City Police Department, that approval for all aspects of the study depended on headquarters accepting the research. It would also be necessary to establish ourselves with the precinct officers with whom we would be interacting on a daily basis. While headquarters' approval was necessary, it would not automatically ensure, and quite possibly might hinder, our acceptance at the precinct level. Not surprisingly, our first experiences with getting official approval indicated the alternate communication structures and lines of communication we found operating throughout the study.

With the approval of the National Institute of Law Enforcement and Criminal Justice, we began the process of getting formal departmental approval for the study and for the selection of the study precincts. A project description was prepared and a letter requesting permission to begin the study was forwarded to the police commissioner, who must approve any research conducted in the department. Some weeks later we received a telephone message that the commissioner did not approve the study. We then turned to the "informal" system by contacting a number of ranking officials in the department whom we knew; they contacted the police commissioner's staff and in a sense "vouched" for us. This approach resulted in our finally being given approval. We were assigned a project monitor in the Office of Programs and Policies and told that we should coordinate the selection of the precincts with the Office of Field Services, which has direct operational control over precincts.

There is a growing body of literature on problems of entry (or access) and maintenance of a credible field presence in any organization over an extended period of time.[1] In studies of police organization or policing this literature most frequently points at problems created by the very strongly felt insider/outsider dichotomy among police personnel. That police personnel always refer to anyone not a "sworn member" of the department as a "civilian" is symbolic of their perceived inhospitality toward outsiders. Through experience in a number of organizational studies we have learned that the management level personnel who agree to the study will usually be cooperative in direct relation to how far removed the research is from their operations. Seemingly, studying "down" in the organizational hierarchy is more difficult to arrange than studying "up." Obviously, management has some vested interest in what a study might be able to tell them about "workers," but less so in what a study might be able to tell them (or anyone else) about what they are doing and how they are doing it. So while we had been given official go-ahead by the police commissioner, we knew that this approval simply permitted us entry and would probably have little influence on our acceptance at the precinct. While some systems might open up to a researcher who comes with the blessing of the "boss," there are probably more systems in which that blessing will be more of a problem than an *entré*. A general rule of thumb is that the greater the distance, in terms of organizational size and complexity, between the level of official endorsement and the locus of the study, the greater the level of suspicion and resistance encountered.

We were interested in discovering basic patterns of social relationships in a precinct no matter where it might be located physically. We had spent a great deal of time trying to decide whether or not it was possible to describe and select a "typical" precinct in which to discover "typical" or basic patterns of relationships. First, we had to define "typical." Various police officers with whom we spoke provided an equally valid, but different set of characteristics for a typical precinct. Important characteristics such as the type and level of crime activity, the socioeconomic status of the community served, demography, ethnic composition of precinct personnel, length of tenure of the commanding officer, and precinct size, were discussed in terms of their relative significance in relation to a description of a typical urban police precinct. We finally decided that for the purposes of our research the search for a typical precinct was a fruitless one. Although we determined that we could not and need not search for several typical or "ideal" precincts, we did feel that it might be profitable to select two precincts which would give us some necessary variety, while avoiding obviously extreme situations.

Aware of the level of suspicion that anyone coming out to the field from central headquarters carried along with their official approval, we simply and straightforwardly explained our research agenda and objectives. We knew that a telephone call to the officers at our field site from officers in the department who had credibility (either through personal acquaintance or sharing a similar function and/or rank in the system, thereby establishing mutual understanding of the problems or threats that our study might pose) would be very helpful in paving our way. Consequently, for this introduction into the field and at several other critical times throughout the life of the study, we were, in a sense, personally vouched for by someone in the system. The key to opening doors was never our professional or formal credentials (degrees, previous research, publications, etc.) but rather the personal trust and camaraderie between fellow officers, one of whom was willing to put that trust on the line to vouch for us. It was a lesson we were to learn over and over again in this organization.

Precinct Selection

At our first meeting with the deputy chief of field services, we described the nature of the study and the general characteristics we were hoping to find in the study precinct. After considerable discussion, including the pros and cons of selecting one of three precincts that the PC had suggested where there were special problems of interest to the department, we agreed that the deputy chief of field services would contact each of the borough or area commanders, inform them of the study, and arrange for us to meet individually to discuss the possibility of specific precincts under their command. We began this process in the Bronx because there were a number of precincts there which met our general requirements.

We were fortunate in that the first borough commander with whom we spoke was enthusiastic, and even encouraging, about our doing the study in "his" borough. Whether this was a function of the objective merits of the study, or of his having advanced degrees and a familiarity with research on policing and with some of our previous research, or of his reputation as an innovative and "intellectual" police administrator who had published several articles on policing, or of some combination of the three, his response was highly supportive. His approval allowed us to move rather easily and quickly to the next level of approval — the precinct. We discussed two precincts and finally decided to go directly to the commanding officer of one and get his reaction to our conducting the study in his command. We had decided, after talking with the deputy chief of field services, that a busy precinct would offer us a vantage point for the widest range of events, operational conditions, and diversity of personnel, and that this Bronx precinct had one of the highest activity levels in the city. The borough commander called the precinct CO, explained who we were and sent us directly to the precinct. While we were at first concerned that we were going to be perceived as having been "shoved-down-his-throat" by a superior, our subsequent experience convinced us that if this precinct commander had not wanted us there he would have politely refused us. We went directly to the station house, met the CO, discussed the study and how we would like to operate in his command. He gave us his approval and turned us over to his administrative lieutenant.

We had decided in advance that the division of labor on the study would be dictated by the desirability of having one of us in continuous presence at the precinct. This meant that one of us should take some role in the precinct which could be carried out by a civilian and which might actually contribute to the work of the precinct, at least in the initial stages of the study. Once having established a presence there, I could gradually begin to accompany officers on a variety of patrol tasks as well as become involved in other aspects of the work of the precinct. At no time did I attempt to disguise the fact that I was conducting a research project at the precinct. We felt that my continuous presence there, working regular shifts and tours, would be the best means of establishing the familiarity and rapport necessary for the study.

While I was establishing my presence in the precinct, Francis Ianni, my coworker, would be observing and interviewing in the community and maintaining contacts at the borough and headquarters levels. We felt that this division of labor would insure one of us becoming a constant participant in the daily life of the precinct without the suspicion and possible contamination which would result from that same person working concurrently at higher levels of the administration. We also felt that the presence of a female was much less threatening and problematic than that of a male might be. (A paradox in a predominantly male society.)

After some consultation with the administrative lieutenant, it was decided that I begin working in the 124 room (an office where complaints of crimes are recorded and where complainants and others call in for information on reported crimes). This office is located on the first floor and very much in the middle of precinct activity and is a good vantage point for much precinct activity. More importantly, it was a good place for officers to get used to me. The 124 room is staffed primarily by civilians although there is usually a police officer on restricted duty assigned there temporarily. My first day in the field was delayed by a week because in the fall of 1976 police officers were demonstrating — threatening strikes and job actions — over contract negotiations with the city. The administrative lieutenant suggested that I hold off a few days until things quieted down and he would have more time to introduce me around the station house. On October 13, 1976, I began observations in this Bronx precinct.

I had intended to spend a few weeks in each of the precinct offices before going out with the patrol force but two fortuitous circumstances developed early in my field presence that changed this intention. Through a project conducted with the NYPD the previous year, I had come to know some officers in other precincts. A few days after beginning work at the precinct, I was approached by two officers (radio car partners) who suggested that whenever I wanted, I could ride with them. Apparently one of the officers whom I had met during the earlier study had worked closely with these two officers and had phoned them saying that I was "o.k." and that they should help me out. These officers were also very helpful because they answered questions immediately raised by the other officers about who I was and what was I doing at the precinct. This vouching for me by the two officers was an invaluable service, not only in this critical beginning phase when I was still unknown at the precinct, but throughout the study. It was fortunate also that this team was well respected in the precinct, since being associated with "nuts" (officers considered different or unusual) could have been disastrous.

The other fortuitous circumstance was that the precinct commanding officer felt comfortable enough with his own control of precinct activity that he allowed me a great deal of latitude and flexibility in movement and in fact signed a memo allowing me access to any police activity within the boundaries of the precinct. I had already signed the required departmental "save-harmless" release absolving them from any responsibility for injuries I might incur while at the precinct.

The Bronx Precinct Community

During the fifteen months in the Bronx precinct community, we became accustomed to its visible representation of the social and physical decay that has come to be associated with the South Bronx. Housing in the area was rapidly disappearing either through abandonment or as a result of the escalating and virtually institutionalized process in which slumlords and/or tenants torched tenements so regularly as to give the area the name "The Arson Capital of the World." The officers at this Bronx precinct recognized the decline and often expressed their certainty that this precinct would follow the pattern of the nearby precinct which had gained notoriety as "Fort Apache" because it was virtually under siege from a surrounding hostile community. Only a few years later, however, it was renamed "Little House on the Prairie" as the surrounding community disappeared due to arson and abandonment. Our precinct included a section that had once been called the "Park Avenue" of the Bronx. By the time of our study, in 1976, the destruction and decay of the neighborhood was such that some of the officers had coined their own affectionate epithet for the precinct community — "Jungle Habitat."[2] For the cops who work in this type of precinct, generally referred to as a "shit house" or "garbage house," a tour of duty includes patrolling debris-littered streets and hallways, burned-out hulks of buildings where emergency calls seem to invariably come from a top floor apartment with a broken elevator, hostile faces, jeering kids, high crime, violence, no decent place to eat, and no where to "let down" and relax in security except in the station house.

While statistics can never adequately describe a community, they can at least set proportions. The 1970 census described this precinct community as a 1.95 square-mile area comprised of 60,414 whites (45.5% of the population), 34,884 blacks (25.8%), 33,698 Hispanics (25.4%), with 3,005 (3.3%) others, many of them Orientals or Indians. By 1977, the population estimate had changed dramatically to 8 percent white, 40 percent black, 50 percent Hispanic, and 2 percent other. Policing and protecting this area is the responsibility of approximately 270 officers, 15 detectives, 18 sergeants, 6 lieutenants, and 2 captains.

For many of the cops, coming to work in this precinct means driving in from upstate New York, usually a 90-minute drive (although any cop will swear he lives only 45 minutes away — even if his travel time is closer to two hours). One of the good things about working here is the station house's ready access to highways out of the city. Commuting distance, toll expenses, and parking facilities close to the station house are part of the reward/punishment system perceived by cops to be part of administrative control. Although parking here is convenient and adjacent to the station house, a cop on occasion will return to his car at the end of the day and find his tires slashed or removed by local youths who have the reputation of being able to strip a car parked on the street in the time it takes the driver to get out and lock the doors. Car pools are common, alleviating some of the financial burden in gas and tolls and some of the exhaustion from a day or night tour either too busy or too slow.

The physical geography of the community is a map of debris; of burned-out apartments; of gutted buildings that landlords have abandoned but where squatters, frequently entire families, live — often without lights, water, or sanitation; and of empty lots piled high with garbage thrown out of windows, and inhabited by rats. Even copper pipes in carefully boarded-up buildings are easy pickings once the building is set afire and the fire department has to break in to put out the flames. It is a community where being inside is no safer than being outside. People living in the same building will break into a neighbor's apartment and move stereos and TVs into their own apartment, and muggers and rapists unscrew hallway bulbs and wait for the very old or the very young to come home. Smoking pot openly on streets, passing a joint back and forth while sitting on a park bench, or just leaning against a building hanging out and drinking beer is the norm. In short, this precinct, this community is everything the stereotype of a poor black and Hispanic ghetto implies, including the few who care about their community, their building, or just their own apartment and the many who do not seem to care anymore, if external signs can be read as internal motives. The cops who work in this precinct have read the external signs of the people who live and work here, placed them in comparative context to their own values and mores, and interpreted them to mean at best a lack of caring about themselves, their families, their children, their homes, even their futures; and at worst open and active hostility directed toward each other, toward the system that provides for many of them, and to anyone who ventures into their neighborhood from outside — especially the police. While one may agree or disagree with this reading of the external signs, their perceptions eloquently describe what they feel it means to work here as a police officer. More specifically, it speaks to the question: What is the importance for the job of an officer being assigned to a precinct which is located in a community that is relatively speaking dirtier, poorer, more hostile, more violent than other precincts in the city to which he might have been assigned, or to which he had once been assigned, or to which friends might currently be assigned? To many of these officers, this is an outpost and so they relate to the surrounding community like an army of occupation.

Frequently, especially in the first weeks at the precinct, I was taken on a "sight-seeing tour" (not because I asked, since I would specifically request that they just go about their business as though I was not there). Buildings were pointed out that as recently as ten years before were carefully landscaped with small bridges crossing ponds, and ducks walking freely in the courtyards. Now there was just dirt and a broken cement hole filled with shattered bottles. Sometimes I was taken into large apartment buildings with barely visible remnants of mosaic tiled floors, floor-to-ceiling mirrors and art nouveau decorations on the ceilings and walls. "This place is a gold mine for an antique store," one officer commented as he pointed out glass door knobs and stained glass windows on the landings. It was not at all unusual, I found, for some of the few remaining decorations to be lovingly "liberated" or removed, cleaned up, and presented to a wife or girlfriend as a gift by one of the officers. When this was done in my presence there was never any attempt to hide or apologize for doing it. It was done as though any reasonable person would understand that such objects were no longer appreciated or valued here and therefore deserved a better fate. Interestingly, this was done quite openly in front of other officers and usually even when patrol sergeants were present, but never when a lieutenant was present.

The most immediate work place for those officers working inside the station house is an old three-story stone building. Inside, the three floors are comprised of various sized offices as well as a detention cell; one small room with a TV, large table, and well worn sofa set aside as the lunch room; and a musty basement with a ping pong table and some gym equipment purchased by the precinct club with funds raised from various social events. While most of the men quickly adjust to these rather grim, colorless rooms, occasionally one of them, usually a younger one or one who has recently been transferred from a newer station house, will comment on the conditions of their working space:

> They talk about taking pride in ourselves, in what we are, ha! They should visit us down here some time, why the hell do they expect me to care about keeping my uniform clean or my shoes polished if they stick me in this filthy hole? [or,] They want me to show respect, how about showing respect for me. . . . Give me a clean locker room.

Another cop commented on the differences of assignment, noting that cops at the 13th precinct in Manhattan, for example, have the police academy in the same building and can use the basketball courts, the gym and its equipment, and the pool whenever they want. One constantly recurring theme was that the department should provide good gym equipment at the station houses because, as more restrictions are placed on the use of guns, many officers feel that increased emphasis should be placed on physical conditioning:

> They make such a big deal about the firearms cycle [Officers of all ranks must qualify at the range twice a year, once at the indoor range and again at the outdoor range], when I don't ever plan to use my gun again unless someone is pointing one at me or my partner, but we all [other cops] could use some physical exercise and I sure as hell am not going to do it on my own time . . . or pay to go to some gym. . . . Some guys have such bellies they could get in real trouble. . . . I don't even mean running to catch some nut . . . I mean running away!

Some of the older cops would then chime in on the use of the night stick:

> In the old days we really used these bats, but these young guys don't know there is a real art to using them. . . . There should be retraining in using them right.

Discussing physical exercise, some of the cops, especially younger ones, felt that it was each guy's responsibility to take care of himself, and in almost all of the cases where they brought it up, their appearance suggested that they did take care to keep in shape. A few of the older cops added jokingly that they expected their younger partners to handle the chases. One lieutenant mentioned:

> The department used to care about being overweight, in fact, you could be passed over on a promotion if you were. . . . Now, the department is just interested in covering themselves in court cases on discrimination . . . and since they couldn't prove that being overweight affected how you did your job . . . now they don't give a damn about that either.

There is an old stove and an even older refrigerator in the basement and occasionally, especially on a late tour or very early Sunday morning, some guys get together, buy groceries, and cook up breakfast for the others who are working. While most of the officers like this and many commented that they missed it since the cops who used to do it regularly were no longer around, it is a tricky business since it means bending the regulations a little. Often it would depend on what boss or supervisor was around or what the chances were of a zone inspector or someone from the borough stopping by the station house. One very real problem to which this bending of the rules and regulations is a response is that there are few restaurants in the area and even fewer that are open during late tour hours, 11:30 p.m. to 7:30 a.m. Departmental regulations governing meals while working require that you not leave the boundaries of the precinct. This is, in fact, enforced rather loosely, but the point is that the restriction is always there if someone wants to crack down. On several occasions I heard the rules and procedures guide explained as "rules and regulations covering everything that they can get us on, but nothing about what the hell we are supposed to really be doing out there," or on occasion, "If they want to get us on something, you can be sure it's written in there somewhere now or they'll add it. So they can catch us tomorrow."

By and large the patrol officers at this precinct see themselves as an occupying army and frequently use the expression as an explanation of how they operate there. The predominately white patrol force continually comments with amazement at the dirt — litter on the streets, in the hallways, elevators and entrances of buildings and in the apartments. What makes this perception even more compelling is the fact that quite a few of the officers, particularly those of Irish or Italian ancestry claim to have been brought up in this same neighborhood or had relatives within the neighborhhood. "We lived right in that building," one of the officers pointed out as we rode by one night, "and we were poor, probably poorer than the people here now because my father was too proud to accept public assistance. . . . We didn't have bikes [He points to the several bikes lying on the pavement in front of the entrance doors] and my grandmother who lived with us was outside here sweeping the front steps every morning — now these people moved in and it looks like a pigsty." Another office commented, "Shit, they don't have to work, can't they at least keep things clean." Perhaps the most important personal effect of this perception of the community was the frequent mention of how ridiculous it was for the department to stress dress and appearance in such an environment:

> They[3] are always hassling us about keeping our hats on and shirts buttoned and then they send us out to muck our way through garbage, broken bottles, and piss . . . and I'm not even talking about alleyways, I'm talking about inside buildings. . . . and duck bricks and bottles heaved from those buildings

[The officer pointed them out as we drove by]. All they care about is that someone might take a picture of one of us with our hats off and our collars open and it would look bad for them.[4]

Much has been written about police prejudice, usually painting a picture of cops as products of lower class, immigrant Irish and Italian families with the attendant conservatism and racial biases, and pointing out that such prejudice comes to the job with the cop as part of this background and upbringing. While this may be so, we found that it is just as obvious that many of the cops' attitudes towards minorities and the poor are simply confirmed by evidence they find in their occupational experience. One frequent and often rhetorical question asked of me by cops was, how could I explain that when their families lived in the neighborhood and they were poor, the streets, houses, and apartments were clean; and now with blacks and Puerto Ricans living in them there is garbage and filth all around. While a significant number immediately answered their own questions by saying that all blacks and Puerto Ricans are dirty, others were equally vehement about a system that "allows people and whole families to stay on the dole generation after generation" or that "The papers don't yell when sanitation men get caught sleeping in the trucks or leave more garbage around than they pick up." They complain about slum landlords who "live on Park Avenue and only come around here in their Cadillacs to pick up the rents." But what bothers officers most are the children. Any number of times when responding with a radio car team to a family dispute at eleven or twelve at night, sleepy-eyed kids stand around watching their mother and father cursing, punching, and abusing each other. Invariably, as we rode down in the elevator, the cops will exclaim, "Those poor kids don't have a chance."

The cops frequently reminisced that only ten years earlier, this was one of the quietest precincts in the Bronx. Usually only two cars would cover the whole precinct; one had the north section, the other the south. Now, I was told by the precinct commander, this precinct has seen its peak in terms of crime activity, and waves of decay, arson, assault, poverty, and despair have swept over it and moved even further north. At best, police effort is a holding action. There is little talk of rebuilding or even restoring. Although President Carter's South Bronx redevelopment project had become a big political plum, its promise was earmarked for an area further to the south. The reaction to the news of the president's South Bronx project, when it was first publicized, was, "They better station tanks around the area; it will go the way of all other great projects to restore blocks or buildings or neighborhoods. A lot of planners get the money, a couple of people get a better apartment for a few weeks, but then the scum bags come back in and within a few months the burnings and strippings and abandonment begin all over again." One cop added resignedly, "Who will be the fall guys? We will, because we are the only ones that are out here twenty-four hours that these people can turn to."

For fifteen months I worked continuous tours — day, night, and late tours both in precinct staff offices and on patrol. I spent time as well with the various special details that work out of the precinct — anticrime, conditions units, warrants, and the precinct detective squad. Although I spent time talking with officers who had steady foot posts or scooter assignments, my feeling was that the confusion engendered by intensive observation of such patrols would not make it worth the effort. I relied on direct interviews of those officers and stories of their activities brought back to the station house. Whenever the borough commander agreed, either Francis Ianni or I attended borough meetings with the commanding officer or the executive officer. This occurred at irregular intervals and there were three different borough commanders during those fifteen months in the Bronx.

After we had been in the Bronx precinct for twelve months we decided (in agreement with the project monitor from the National Institute of Law Enforcement and Criminal Justice and the NYPD monitor) that we should spend a shorter period of time in another precinct which would offer some comparison to the Bronx precinct. Our request came just at the time of the appointment of a new police commissioner, which meant changes in the command of various administrative offices which had to approve our request. The system held true to its bureaucratic ideal. A change in top level personnel results in the system in effect stopping, and everyone scrambling to hold on to their current assignment, or maneuvering to move to a preferred one; consequently I spent about three more months at the Bronx precinct waiting for approval of my move to a second precinct. I began working in the second precinct on March 7, 1978.

The Manhattan Precinct Community

When we mentioned the Manhattan precinct where we intended conducting the second phase of our study to several cops in the Bronx precinct, one laughed and said, "If I got transferred there, I would think I had died and gone to heaven." This was a fairly typical comment on how cops from the Bronx viewed the difference between assignment to their precinct and the Manhattan precinct. Everything that was lacking in the Bronx was (abundant) in Manhattan — at least in their perception. One sergeant commented (with nods of agreement from officers standing around) that if he were assigned to that Manhattan precinct, "I would be getting a divorce for sure." There was another side to the advantages of working in an area renowned for good-looking women, excellent restaurants, and future job possibilities through connections made in the area. Some cops said that in such a politically important area (because of wealthy influential people who lived and/or worked there) "the bosses are always breathing down your neck. . . . At least here [at the Bronx precinct] they know you're busy and let you alone." One cop who had worked in a similar Manhattan precinct noted, "There's no camaraderie in those places. . . . You have to look out for yourself. . . . No one will back you up there. It's actually more dangerous because you get sloppy. . . . Things don't happen all the time so you forget to look over your shoulder. You forget to look out for your partner . . . and that's when you get hurt."

"Goodies" does not adequately describe the glamour and wealth that reside in this 1.26 square-mile area of luxury townhouses, embassies, and high-rise apartments protected by twenty-four-hour doormen and closed-circuit TV monitored hallways and elevators. The safety of its 147,000 residents is the responsibility of 236 police officers, 11 detectives, 17 sergeants, 4 lieutenants, and 2 captains.

The community has approximately 93 percent white, 1 percent black, and 4 percent Hispanic residents. While the cops who do not work there see the glamour of a community comprised of airline stewardesses, wealthy and bored divorcees, expensive restaurants, and businessmen with "big bucks," officers who work in this command more often speak of the lack of respect by these people, "who treat you like you are some kind of lackey, who don't want their neighbors to see you come in because it is bad for their reputation or bad for business." While an assignment to guard a consulate used to be an unwanted assignment given to junior men, today there is an embassy detail worked by cops who are willing to accept the routine and boredom of standing outside the door of a consulate for days on end, for regular working hours, in exchange for not having to work around the clock. During the day the many boutiques and restaurants are filled with shoppers from around the world and the streets are usually so packed with cars and taxi cabs that the cops say you get around better on foot. "God help someone who had to get to a hospital quickly," although there are several hospitals within the boundaries of the precinct.

"Burglar alarms are our biggest headache," said one cop who has spent many years at this command. "Almost every other call is an unfounded burglar alarm. . . . The alarm companies find it cheaper to have us respond than to fix the damn things." The time spent unnecessarily by radio cars responding to alarms that go off by accident because of malfunctions, or just because an employee forgets to turn it off before he opens the store in the morning, has become so costly in man-hours that one officer with previous experience in installing burglar alarms spends his whole tour checking out repeated unfounded occurrences and contacting the owner of the business and/or the alarm company to politely suggest that they had better do something to repair their system. This is not a unique police prob-

lem in major urban areas, and in some cities police departments have begun charging store owners for the equivalent response time of officers, if an
alarm goes off due to malfunction or misuse.

Many of the cops assigned here complain, sometimes bitterly, about the
"crap we have to take from people who think they are better than we are
. . . and we have to take it because you know damn well they will be on the
phone to someone at city hall who they are friends with and we'll get a
complaint." One cop went so far as to suggest (with colleagues nodding
agreement) that this command should be considered "high hazard" because of the trouble a guy can get into just for not watching his language.
Another cop who happened to have spent a few years at the Bronx precinct
added another perspective when he commented that, "At least over there if
a guy gives you trouble you can tell him where to go and you won't get any
flack over it from him or the bosses . . . because they understand that kind
of language. . . . Over here, you have to learn a completely new language."

A sergeant told us, "The boss [the precinct commanding officer] here
has to spend most of his time massaging the important people in the community. He has to be a real diplomat because they sure know how to use
their phones and who to call to get action." Another cop embellished this
theme with, "And here they don't just call the precinct when they want
some action or have some complaint . . . they write a Dear Abe [the
mayor] or Dear Mike [the PC] . . . and they can get away with it."

Physically, the station house itself is not much newer than the one in the
Bronx, but the precinct club has been able to set up a very elaborately
equipped gym in the basement for the officers, and the eating room has a
pool table and color television. While the Bronx station house is home, a
place of refuge from the dirt and community resentment perceived just
outside the door and consequently a place always filled with officers on and
off duty (unless someone from the borough command happens to be visiting), in Manhattan there is much more on the outside to interest a cop and
consequently much less hanging around inside the station house. Even eating is a matter of personal finances and having to choose among some of
the finest, albeit expensive restaurants in the world.

A good deal of the police job here has to do with making certain that an
individual is covered for insurance purposes when a theft or burglary has
occurred, or, with increasing frequency, when someone's car is stolen or
vandalized. Some of the cops told us that there is an increase in crime in
this area because the "mutts from up north or from the Bronx have heard
about the good pickings here," and much of the time of anticrime teams is
spent watching for, and following, groups of black or Hispanic kids that
wander the streets "until they get on the subway and get out of here or
cross over into the next precinct and become their problem." Black and
Hispanic youth are unusual enough in this neighborhood to stand out and

they usually are only here to cause trouble," said one anticrime cop. On a particularly quiet night cars with several blacks or Hispanics might be followed until they cross out of the precinct boundaries.

A frequent complaint among the cops here is the problem of parking the cars they drive in to work. There used to be a parking lot around the corner, but construction was begun there a few years ago (and left unfinished). Now it is first come, first served along several of the streets around the station house, but not enough to accommodate all of the cars. Free and convenient parking is expected as a job benefit and it becomes the basis of hard feelings and even union action because there is always another precinct that is pointed out as having more convenient and readily available parking.[5]

Another frequently heard complaint is, "Around here, appearance is important to the bosses. You better have your shoes shined and your hat on when you get out of your car." From observations over the several months spent there, this concern seemed to be more theoretical than factual, and physical appearance was more directly related to a guy wanting "to look sharp for the girls around here" than to please the bosses or comply with regulations. Several of the men noted that there were more divorced cops at this precinct, than any other in the city. I was unable to verify this, but the implication was that the temptations abounding in these few miles of blocks were formidable. Certainly, there were more than a few occasions when I saw officers make new contacts just by pulling up alongside an attractive girl and suggesting that they get together later — asking and, more often than not, getting phone numbers and addresses. "Girls think we are safe," was a common explanation for their success with women. One cop and his partner seem to agree that airline stewardesses were particularly attracted to cops because, "They run into trouble often with kooks that they meet on planes or just hanging around in bars when they are in town, and they like the fact that we carry guns. They know even if they can't reach us, they can usually get one of our buddies who might be working when they need help quick and quiet."

"Discount buying" is one of the advantages of getting to know some of the shopkeepers, especially in an area where most of the cops said that they could not afford to buy the things in those stores even on sale. Despite departmental integrity programs and strict regulations, free meals and drinks in local establishments are not an uncommon occurrence. "One hand washes the other" is a commonly heard expression regarding such matters. "Downtown doesn't really care about little stuff like free eats or drinks," one cop said, "as long as it's kept quiet so that they aren't embarrassed." He went on to explain, "They are usually just interested in catching us on big stuff. They have been pretty successful in controlling that only because they have made it so that no one trusts the next guy . . . and you can't get very big on your own." In fact, only several weeks after I arrived there, I was told by three different cops that I should not use the phone on the corner, or the phone in the muster room. The implication was that both phones were bugged by headquarters — a reputation that probably goes back to the time of the Knapp Commission investigation when several precinct phones had, according to rumor, been monitored.

Community relations at the Manhattan precinct is a regular assignment for one officer and a continuous headache for the precinct commanding officer. "The only time you get a big turnout at community meetings," I was told, "is over an issue like prostitutes hanging out in a certain area, or a bar or a club that plays music too loud, or kids hanging around." Cops were resentful of the fact that "many people who have been robbed or whose apartments have been burglarized don't really even want the police to do anything. . . . Many even refuse to take the time to go to court when a suspect is caught, because it's all insured so they don't really give a damn. . . . All they want is a complaint number for their insurance."

On the other hand, because of the influence of many people residing in the precinct, even relatively minor occurrences will be given special treatment, such as assigning a detective to go to a home and speak with the complainant even on a relatively minor incident. "Not that it means anything," one detective explained, "but they expect this kind of treatment because of who they are and not because they see it on the police shows on TV. We give it to them because of the trouble they can cause us."

The Field Data

During the 18 months of the study, I spent a total of 168 eight-hour tours of duty in both precincts. Of these 168 tours, 120 were in the Bronx precinct and the remaining 48 were in the Manhattan precinct. The tours of duty in both precincts included working with and observing in the 124 or complaint room, with the precinct investigation unit (PIU), and the various patrol units, community relations and other staff units inside the station house. We maintained contact and carried out interviews with the commanding officers of both precincts as well as other administrative personnel at both the precinct and area or borough command levels. At various times during the study we interviewed personnel at police headquarters as well as a number of former officers of the department. In total, we were in contact with 310 police officers of all ranks, currently or formerly associated with the two precincts. The degree of contact varied from casual conversation, either on duty or in the various formal or informal social gatherings held by the precincts, to extensive and continuous contact with officers of various ranks in each of the precincts. I rode with many of the radio car teams in both precincts but spent far more time with a smaller number of teams in order to observe some continuity of police work. Observations were carried out during all tours, on weekends and holidays as well as during the week.

The result of these observations and interviews was thousands of pages of field notes as well as a considerable volume of archival and documentary material. Presenting these data in some form which is both faithful to the field situation and indicative of the social structure of the precinct is a problem which confronts all field studies. We used events as the focal point for observation and interviewing since we wanted to look at the social action which generates and displays that social organization rather than to deal with more static notions such as role, status, attitude, or motivation.

The Events

We came upon the notion of the opposition of street cop culture and management cop culture through the process of continuously analyzing and categorizing the field data as it was collected. In the sense that I use event analysis, a particular event becomes the focal point for the collective interpretation of social and behavioral processes illustrative of attitudes, behaviors, and motivations of the street cop culture.

The next section contains a description of four events that took place during our presence at the two precincts: the trial of an officer accused of killing a suspect while under police custody, the suicide of a policeman under department investigation for alleged illegal activity, the attempt by headquarters management to implement a management-by-objectives program in the precinct, and a citywide electrical blackout. I chose these events not because of the particular action or drama involved in each, but because each generated sufficient activity and reaction to provide the opportunity for focalized, event-generated observation, interviewing, and analysis. They illustrate and explicate the process and meaning of the underlying conflict between the two cultures of policing.

Each of the events is fairly dramatic and succeeded in clarifying a number of the social and behavioral relationships and processes I had seen in observing routine activity and had heard in conversation in the precincts. In describing the events and the reaction to these events, I have tried to follow linkages which each event made obvious, as well as to relate some of the field data which I had gathered from more routine events observed on a daily basis. Obviously, there is some overlap among the four events since social organization, social networks, rules, and organizational processes, while they may be analytically separable, are operationally interactive. It is also telling that certain themes were continuously present in response to quite different events.

Notes

1. See Manning (1976), and Lundman and Fox (1974) for a fuller discussion of this problem.
2. Jungle Habitat was the name of a wild animal park open to the public in northern New Jersey which has since gone out of business.
3. This generalized "they" is usually used in a pejorative sense to refer to bosses or superiors or officers working inside jobs at central headquarters. It is not, however, unique to policing. Crozier (1964), for example, notes "significantly, complaints are never directed at specific individuals, but towards management or toward the still vaguer 'they' " (p. 13).
4. Such an incident actually occurred in a Bronx precinct. A documentary had been filmed at a precinct showing police operations in the street and at the station house. The documentary was very realistic, showing a homicide and including street language by the police as well as the citizens. During the first showing of the film on television, the borough commander had telephoned into the station house, we were told, "demanding to know the names of the officers who were seen without their hats on or their collars buttoned."
5. This expectation of certain "perks" (i.e., perquisites) that go with the job is not unique to the police in New York City. Teachers, for example, expect to be able to park near their schools, firemen near their fire stations, etc.

CHAPTER 4
The Trial of Officer Kelly

In the summer of 1975, a 25 year old male Hispanic was arrested in his apartment by police officer Michael Kelly, charged with assault and robbery, and brought into the Bronx precinct station house. Some hours later he was removed by ambulance from the station house and taken to a nearby hospital. He died five hours later of a ruptured spleen. The police officer who had arrested this man was subsequently charged with murder and two years later, after being dismissed from the department, was convicted of criminally negligent homicide and sentenced to four years in prison. He was the first New York City police officer to be tried for the murder of a prisoner while in police custody.

Headlines in the *New York Post* of November 7, 1977, read in bold black type, "Killer Cop Jury Torn by Strife." The story to all appearances was straightforward. Police officers were directed to the door of an apartment in the Bronx by a burglary suspect. When the police knocked at the apartment door, shots were fired through the door from inside the apartment. Several officers broke through the door and Officer Kelly wrestled with the suspect in an effort to restrain him. The suspect was questioned in the apartment as to the whereabouts of the gun that had been used to fire through the door at the police. Present in the apartment were the suspect's wife who was eight months pregnant, a female friend, the patrol sergeant, and several officers, including Officer Kelly. The suspect was removed to the station house under arrest. The allegations were that the arresting officer had beaten the suspect while in the apartment and subsequently beat him further in the second floor squad room of the precinct causing his death. The prisoner died in the hospital several hours later.

This event was selected for analysis because in one sense it represents an almost classic case of the street cop culture in conflict with the management cop culture and of conflicting codes of behavior and interpretations.

It points as well to the manner in which management culture is destroying the traditional street cop culture. It pitted cop against cop in order to fix the blame for the death of the prisoner. Seven cops eventually testified against Kelly admitting that they had lied during the initial grand jury investigation, allegedly to protect him, explaining that it was an accepted practice to commit perjury to help a fellow officer. At the trial, six officers, including the patrol sergeant, testified they had seen Kelly kick and beat the suspect in the apartment, in the squad room, and in the bathroom of the station house. Kelly, on the other hand, claimed that he had been made the scapegoat for fellow cops who had been forced to "make deals" to save their jobs and pensions. He insisted that other officers had a hand in the beating of the suspect. In his final presentation to the jury the defense attorney, a well-known criminal lawyer who had successfully defended another officer charged with homicide in an earlier case, portrayed Kelly as a courageous officer — a "Jack Armstrong," an all-American boy, a "Mr. Applepie and football," — while the prosecution claimed the officer had "acted with completely depraved indifference to human life."

Although the actual arrest and subsequent death of the prisoner occurred prior to my being at the precinct, the trial took place during the study. The elements of conflict that surrounded the case and the reactions of the precinct officers throughout the several weeks of the trial provided me with an ideal opportunity to observe the dynamics of the organizational conflict. While it was in one sense a unique event, it exposed the possibility of such an occurence in the day-to-day work of policing. A number of officers commented, "It could have happened to any of us."

The facts of the event were as presented in the news media. There were, however, symbolic conflicts in the interpretation of these facts. To the Hispanic community, the victim, regardless of his notoriety as a drug dealer, was one of their own and represented the poverty and powerlessness of urban ghetto life face to face with "the man," police brutality, and prejudice. To police headquarters and the political administration it served, there was all of the anxiety surrounding media exposure of a distasteful trial during a mayoral election year, pressure from downtown, and questions of responsibility and accountability to the community and to the image of the department. To the cops in the Bronx precinct, there were also conflicting issues: loyalty and camaraderie, "them against us " ("them" being the "bosses" and city hall, as well as the community), the accountability and authority of supervisors, questions of discretion in police work, job-related stress and tension, and "Monday morning quarterbacking" by everyone else. While the event was unique, the conflicts and issues it exposed were integral to the daily experiences of the precinct and of street cops.

Public Relations: Events that create bad publicity activate management cop culture to do something about what they see as out-of-control street cop culture.

Newspaper coverage of the trial was extensive and dramatic. On November 7, 1977, the headline in the *New York Post*, "Killer Cop Jury Torn by Strife" had been followed by a lengthy story entitled "Cops Beat Prisoners, A Detective Admits at Kelly's Murder Trial." Such headlines caused immediate and widespread anger at the station house during the trial, although it was a restrained, almost resigned anger. "You never hear anything good about us," one officer said. "I guess it doesn't sell papers because it isn't sensational." Another cop pointed out that when ordinary citizens are involved in wrong-doings, they "don't put that person's job title up front." Another commented, "We are all different, only when something bad is reported, it's bad for all of us. . . . The same thing happened during Knapp when the amount of money cops were taking was reported all over the place. . . . Even my wife looked at me funny . . . like she thought I had been holding out on her all those years. . . . and I have a neighbor who still asks me where I have it hidden." He laughed adding "I'd like to belt him, but sure as anything the papers would report that a cop had belted his neighbor."

Many of the officers noted a direct relationship between poor press and headquarters response. "Even headquarters thinks we're all alike," was the topic of discussion one evening while I was riding with two officers on patrol. "If something happens in Brooklyn, sure enough an order will come down to every command in the city even if the situation barely applied in the Bronx." His partner added, "Yeah, it's like they always want to be sure they've covered themselves, like in the patrol guide. . . . It's against the rules, but everyone is doing it and everyone knows that it's being done everywhere, but it's there just in case they want to get you." This view of headquarters — "Always out to screw you while protecting their own ass" — was one of the most frequently heard complaints during the eighteen month study, in both precincts.

Concern over exploitation of the police by reporters was often cited as a major reason for turning off to all civilians. In many cases this included both of us, at least until we came to be accepted in the precinct. Unless an officer in the precinct (or an officer from another precinct) could vouch for us, each new personal encounter was guarded and we were continuously tested. One night, for example, I was riding in a radio car with cops who were not usually teamed together. One of the team was an officer with whom I had ridden before; the other officer was just filling in while his regular partner was out sick. The new officer said immediately that he was not going to talk to me and would not have let me ride if this had been his car, but he had gone along with the officer who knew me and had decided not to make an issue of my presence for the tour. Several hours into the tour, probably because he began to see the other officer was being relatively open and frank in his discussion of various topics, he told the story of a previous experience with a female reporter. This experience had led him to vow never to allow any civilian in his car. The department has approved a female reporter to ride in the precinct, and she had been placed in the radio car with him and his partner. The three of them had gotten on very well and by the end of the week they felt comfortable enough to really begin to talk to her about what they felt was "the real picture." "We trusted her," he emphasized. On their last tour of her assignment with them, she had a camera and said that she wanted to get some good action shots. She also offered to take some just for fun and they could take those home to their families. "We were goofing around," the officer continued. And in that mood she said, "Why don't you two hold hands on the dashboard . . . just for laughs." "Of course," he said, "when the article came out, there was a picture of the two of us, like two fags holding hands and we never heard from her again, and we didn't get any of the other pictures she had promised us either."

Frequently, when complaining about negative press, officers would add, "And the PC never comes out to defend us or explain our side of the story." One officer added, "It's like if he throws us to the wolves he'll come out looking like Mr. Clean." Another officer repeated the frequent refrain, "You can't get your nose dirty working downtown." A third officer added, "Yeah, and those guys sitting up there with their stars and three piece business suits, you know what they were doing when they were out here on the streets." Everyone laughed and nodded.

> *Solidarity and Silence:* Management cop culture demands a watch-dog system that can uncover and expose any internal wrongdoing or corruption and so protect its public image. The street cop culture demands that its activities are closed to external scrutiny from a public that cannot understand the necessity for certain shortcuts because of the nature of the job.

One of the major controversies surrounding the trial, which continuously came up in discussions during that time with officers at the precinct, was the "cop's code" to not inform on a brother officer. It had been reported at the trial that, "It was a well-known fact that cops will lie to protect or cover for one another." It was this code of silence, well documented in police literature, which was said to have led the officers who were witnesses to the events in the apartment and during the interrogation in the station house to deny to the grand jury having seen Kelly brutalizing the suspect, only to recant their testimony at the trial. Regardless of their motives in changing their testimony, this code and the repercussions of their having violated it or "turned-around" are important to understanding the bonds among officers in the street cop culture and the conflicts that result when there is no longer unanimous support of the code.

The patrol sergeant, who was present in the apartment that night, testified at the trial that it is common practice among police officers to lie to grand juries to help a fellow officer. He admitted that he had lied to a grand jury when he denied that he had seen Kelly beat the prisoner, adding that he had lied on other occasions to cover up for fellow officers. Many officers acknowledged to me a long established tradition in the department of "covering" for a fellow officer in trouble. The tradition of the old days held that a "good guy," no matter what, stuck by his colleagues. The folklore suggests that it almost invariably worked because, "If everyone sticks to the same story . . . they can't break you because you know you can trust everyone else to say the same thing." But we were told over and over again (the assertion always illustrated with examples of actual experience) that in reaction to the Knapp report on corruption, the department has instituted an internal security system that "destroys trust and undermines your faith in fellow cops," and consequently the code of silence is threatened.

The Internal Affairs Division (IAD) is the internal security system designed, say the cops, to protect the department and the police commissioner from embarrassing revelations of misconduct. As part of its ongoing investigative network throughout the department, internal affairs uses a group of officers assigned as field associates and placed under cover in field units, including precincts, without the knowledge of the unit or of the precinct commander. These officers perform duties as though they were regularly assigned officers, but in addition, they are responsible for reporting to internal affairs any infraction of the rules by department personnel. Precinct cops consider such cops "turnarounds" (i.e., traitors) and believe that many of them are cops who got "jammed up" through some offense and have accepted this assignment in lieu of harsher disciplinary measures. "They're controlled from downtown," said one supervisor in the precinct. "Even the CO [of the precinct] doesn't know who they are." They also maintain that some of the officers who accept such assignments are recruited directly from the police academy before they develop loyalty to the cop culture. The cops' bemused response is, "Bullshit, there haven't been any academy classes coming out for years." Others suggest that cops accepting such assignments are "mavericks who just can't fit in with the guys." One field training officer told me:

> Nowadays you walk into the lunch room and the conversations just aren't what you used to hear in the old days . . . or two guys are talking to each other and just stop talking when someone else comes in. Guys just don't trust

the other guys the way they used to. Plus there is always the possibility that a field associate is around. In fact, they told us directly that those guys would be around. I had a guy that I was training. This guy thought he was Adam-12 . . . he was a real gung-ho cop. He was so bad that I wrote him up, and I sure as hell think twice before doing something like that to a guy. I found out later that this guy became a field associate.

While the original intention of field associates may have been to seek out graft and corruption in the field (a task which seems to have been accomplished with some success) the side effect, say the cops, is that "You can't trust anybody anymore because IAD has to get on the sheet too. If they can't find anybody going for the big stuff, they'll turn you in for getting a second cup of coffee free on a meal break." The effects of this internal spy system, say the cops, is that while it provides some departmental benefits in funneling information on "little stuff," such as knocking off extra time from the job, "cooping" (sleeping during duty tours), "discount shopping," or getting free meals, it has had a devastating effect on morale.

A question frequently heard in the station house during the trial was: Why had Kelly's fellow officers "ratted" on him and testified for the prosecution? Word at the precinct was that the officers had made deals with headquarters and the prosecution. While they were collectively exempted from prosecution, each, it was said, got something special as well. One cop had been laid off as a result of the budget cuts but was called back before a number of other laid-off cops who had seniority ("jumped up the list"); the patrol sergeant had been ready to retire and was allowed to do so with his full pension; and a detective who had testified was going to retire ("go out on three-quarter's" pay) on a job-related disability. Whatever the reality of these rumors, which were told as absolute fact via the grapevine, they indicated how important it was to explain away the defections from the code on the basis of some strong pressure or personal gain. It was the strength of the bond among brother officers, a pattern of mutual dependence, with the strength and character of kinship, reaching out to the police family, which had been threatened. Regardless of the guilt or innocence of Kelly, it was necessary to explain away the disloyalty of the turnarounds. This social bond has its origins in street cop culture; the ethic of unquestioning support of fellow officers based on the shared dangers of the job. It has grown, however, to include the notion of shared guilt when procedures or even laws have to be bent a little in order to accomplish some aspect of social or collective good. The turnaround cops in the Kelly case brought into question not only their own character and motivation but the strength of group loyalty and the salience of mutual trust. To a working cop in the street, we were told, this further eroded the certainty of support he could expect of his partner and other officers who are "out there." It was extended to imply that cops would now be less willing to take chances and face danger, lacking the certainty that other cops would risk their lives for them. It also meant you would have to "go by the book" and this, so the cops believed, reduces police effectiveness. The term which is used to describe this mutual dependence is "backing up." At one level this means physically arriving on the scene although the job has been assigned to another car, in order to lend extra support; but "backing up" has a shared, more figurative meaning, at the level of group and individual support, no matter what the situation or what might be at stake. To the extent that this mutual support ethic is being eroded, cops believe that their effectiveness is being diminished.

Throughout the study we were told by officers in both precincts that, "Guys won't back you up anymore."

The Kelly trial produced constant and widespread discussion of "backing up" in the Bronx. Such discussions always included agreement on numerous examples of how the job has changed because "you don't know who you can trust anymore." So increasingly you trust fewer and fewer. One officer summed it up by stating, "Now I feel I can only count on my partner, a couple of the guys in my squad, and that's it. I don't even talk much about my business anymore while I'm riding home [in a car pool]." Another officer with over twenty years on the job said that there was mutual support among all of the officers regardless of rank if "anything heavy came down . . . from outside or even from downtown."

> Then, it got to where I felt that only this precinct was a home and the family was here, and you just didn't have much to do with guys you don't know from other precincts. Now there are only a handful of guys here that I will talk to, even guys I have known since I've been on the job because I just don't know who I can trust anymore. Now I have to be concerned for my family, for my wife, my kids and my pension. It's a shame, but I give back what I get.

Conversation with and among officers was filled with references to this perceived change in the department. Usually ending with some variant on the phrase, "So the hell with the job, I'll put my time in, take my pension and run." While I heard these comments most frequently and most forcefully during the trial, it was a usual comment throughout the study: "Now, I just put in my eight hours, get out of my uniform and go home. That's what they've made this job." Some cops suggested that the department was probably quite pleased with such attitudes and perhaps even fostered them. "It's the enthusiastic cop . . . the go-getter that might get into the kind of situation that the department doesn't want to hear about any more . . . that might cause eyebrows to be raised at city hall, or community groups to phone some politician." An older officer added, "Hell, they are talking about us not having to wear our guns all the time, but you can be damn sure it isn't because they see it as a problem for us. It's because they have counted up the number of off-duty shooting incidents, and don't like the results for the image of the department."

While there was general condemnation and much open score expressed during the trial for the turnaround cops, a number of cops confided that they could understand how it could happen nowadays. Several officers expressed open, if guarded, concern — even pity — for the officers because they had been threatened with losing their pensions, "and that's all we have left in this shit job." They also pointed out that "downtown can really lean on you" when they question an officer who will not testify: "Not only threats but treating you like a criminal and not even letting you go to the bathroom alone." "The way this job is going," said one cop, "a smart guy has to look out for himself, even if it also means that he can't look out for the next guy."

Despite these expressions of understanding, the turnaround cops were placed under strong social pressure from other precinct officers. When they returned from court they walked the gauntlet. It was not uncommon for some of the cops standing outside the station house to spit contemptuously as they walked by. No one spoke to them as they walked into the station house, and there were dire predictions about what would happen to them, or to their lockers, and there were rumors that they would be transferred immediately for their own protection.

None of the predictions came true, and the turnarounds remained at their regular jobs in the precinct. This was explained by some cops as the result of the fact that shortly after the trial, the assistant district attorney who prosecuted Kelly had come into the station house and announced to the entire command that if they gave the officers who testified against Kelly any trouble, he (the ADA) would personally see to it that they would be brought up on charges.

One officer who had been present during this incident said, "There is all this bullshit in the court and in the papers now about Kelly killing this guy because he's Puerto Rican. When they were bringing him (the Hispanic suspect) out Kelly was yelling 'you son-of-a-bitch, you'll never shoot at another cop again.'" We heard from several other officers that this was the real issue and that if the man arrested had been white or black, the attitude would have been the same. One night while talking to a group of officers, one officer with eighteen years on the job summed up the traditional feeling of mutual protection.

> In the old days, you just didn't get away with killing a cop . . . like now. Even if the courts had been turnstyles, sending guys out as fast as we send them in, the scumbag who shot at a cop wouldn't get a second chance. Even before he

got to the station house, the guys would have gotten a piece of him. I remember their taking one guy up to the roof and holding him over the edge by his feet. He got the message. He wouldn't ever shoot at another cop.

While traditions of loyalty and silence were expected to cover this case, there were things about Kelly and about the incident that confused their application and indicated some of the conditional aspects of the code today. Officer Kelly had a mixed personal appeal and reputation among the cops at the precinct. He had been at the precinct only four months before the incident occurred but he was well known there. He had come in as a trainee several years earlier before going to another precinct on his first assignment. Several of the officers who remember him from those days said that he was always a trouble maker, and "crazy." "He could always be counted on to find trouble." To other cops in the precinct, especially to the younger ones, he was a real "cop's cop." What that meant to them was that he embodied everything that a "real" cop should be: He was a tough, good looking, playboy, who hung out with other cops at cop bars and hangouts, was aggressive in policing, and "wouldn't hesitate to jump in to help another cop." However, regardless of personal feelings there was always a big show of solidarity for him. Officers rushed over to him, crowded around him, slapped him on the back, and offered words of encouragement when he stopped by the station house at the end of a day at court. He, in turn, was always jovial and confident on these occasions. During one such occasion, an older officer who had been telling me about some of Kelly's "crazy" behavior, got called into one of the back rooms by a group of four young officers and told that he should not be telling me such bad things about Kelly. When he returned he said that he told them that I was all right and that he could tell me anything he wanted. Their reply had been that "only cops understand cops" and that he was taking a chance when he so openly criticized Kelly in front of me. Later, when I asked some of the cops I knew well why there had not been the expected retribution and more hostility shown towards the turnaround cops still at the precinct, they reported that it was because so many of the guys had negative feelings about Kelly, that he was known to be a "brute," and that some of the officers felt that he had been wrong to "bring this kind of publicity down on us." One officer said that he blamed Kelly for the problem because the turnarounds had merely been unfortunate to have been caught by a system which, "once it decides it wants to get you, can do it." Group loyalty is weakening. In the old days the system would have protected and supported the cop against the outside; today, we were told, "You're on your own."

Group Identification: Management cop culture is responsive to new political and social pressures and so is no longer responsive to the old department politics or "old boy" networks. Street cop culture fights against the changes in the game and increases the difficulty of introducing new personnel into precincts.

While the Kelly trial had a tendency to fit all of the cops in the precinct into "loyal" and "turnaround" categories, the event also brought other dimensions of how officers are sorted — by themselves as well as the other officers — into distinctive groupings. We found, in both precincts that the important dimensions of sorting tend to be age, sex, length of service, race, ethnicity, specialized expertise, connections, and behavior under fire. The distinctions on length of service and age are generally quite straightforward in setting up a series from "rookie" to "old timer." There are other age-graded distinctions as well. Some police academy classes, for example, have had a reputation for being full of "crazies" while others are known for having a good group spirit. Within the precinct these distinctions account for differential assignment and respect. Race and ethnicity have some important and yet confusing effects on sorting in the precinct.

An article in the *New York Times* of November 6, 1977 noted that, "The Kelly case, in which the officer is white and the suspect a Puerto Rican, was one of a number in recent years to raise the issue of alleged fatal police brutality by white officers against black or Hispanic people, and the first of those to result in conviction." The issue of minority relations among officers in the precinct, is as much a question of the social organization of the precinct as it is the relationship between white cops and black or Hispanic citizens. Police officers of all ranks but especially at the higher ranks are overwhelmingly white and are still predominantly Irish or Italian. There are, of course, numbers of Jewish or German-American police officers as well as a scattering of other ethnicities, but the Irish and Italians still predominate. In the post–civil rights era, the department has attempted to significantly increase its recruitment among blacks and Hispanics. While this affirmative action is taken seriously at headquarters and city hall, it tends to be less than popular in the field. With increased emphasis on professionalism and higher educational standards in the police community, minority recruitment seems counterproductive because it requires the acceptance of officers with lower educational credentials. It is not the lower educational standards that the older cops complain about, however, but rather it was their contention that minority recruitment means accepting officers with prior criminal records. They quickly pointed out that what might read on one's record as a misdemeanor, frequently was plea-bargained down from a felony. Occasionally, some cops will complain about the lowered height requirements, usually associated with minority recruitment. But this is usually said humorously in the presence of a short

Irish or Italian cop. It was not uncommon to hear cops complain of the very difficult background investigation they had to pass to come on the job. "Nowadays, any mutt can become a cop." In the same context, I also heard cops add, "and he's a guy I might have to depend on someday."

Ethnic sorting shapes some of an officer's personal experience in the precinct but there is a more important relationship with how networks are formed and how these networks relate to the power and authority structure. The NYPD has a long and complex history of the power and influence of various ethnic and religious associations. While Irish Catholic power is still believed to control the authority structure of the department, Italians have been increasing in power because of numbers and upward mobility in the department. Currently, the president of the Patrolman's Benevolent Association (traditionally an Irish position) is an Italian-American. There is a very rich and irreverent vocabulary employed in the constant banter among cops about each other's ethnic heritage. While it may be argued that the frequency and sharpness of the ethnic insults bespeak deeper levels of hostility, our impression is that humor and camaraderie are the more important motives. Racial or ethnic epithets are obviously and openly hostile, however, when an officer deviates from the conventions of cop culture and, in losing his group identification, becomes a "nigger" or a "Jew bastard." This hostility is also apparent when power cliques in the precinct or in the department are being discussed.

The distinctions between older officers who were actually in the department in the good old days and younger officers are apparent. Whenever there is a discussion of "hooks" or "rabbis," older officers always cite ethnic networks within the department as "taking care of their own." One older cop at the precinct told me, "It used to be if you wanted something, you went to the Holy Name breakfast, you talked to someone, and he said, 'Okay, we'll take care of it.' A couple of weeks later you got a telephone message on a 90-day transfer and that got extended and extended and pretty soon everybody forgot you were there temporarily or where you should be and there you were." He went on to add, "And it used to be if you got into trouble or you got brought up on charges, if you have the right connections, the right rabbi, something could be done about it." For younger cops, however, ethnicity seems less important than job-related linkages. These are formed while classmates at the police academy, while working together in a precinct, particularly in the first assignment out of the academy, and while working as partners at some time in their career. When a new police commissioner was appointed during the study, we were told to watch who a new chief would bring with him to his assignment and note in how many cases the staff officers selected by the new chief had worked with him in the old days when they were sergeants or lieutenants together because their loyalties had been tested.

In 1971 the Career Path Program was developed by the department with the intention of eliminating the "hook" or "rabbi" system, and introducing a "sound and comprehensive personnel management system for the assignment and advancement of officers." It prescribed a career path for officers to insure that an officer's career would include assignment to a variety of precincts of both high and low activity, to specialized units, and to investigative units. It stated that advancement would be based on a variety of experiences. Officers with whom I spoke in both precincts were critical and skeptical about the Career Path Program. The 1976 fiscal crisis in New York City and the subsequent layoffs of police officers slowed down and virtually stopped movement to new assignments. The career path was effectively frozen. Everyone with whom I spoke believed that the "hook" or "contract" was still at work in preferential assignments. An officer in the Bronx precinct, who had applied for transfer to a specialized street crime unit, went through all the proper procedures and had been interviewed. When he checked back to see what was happening, he was told by one of the officers in that unit, "If you could just have someone call over for you."

One night while I was riding with an anticrime team, the officers stopped to talk with another team about a former member of the unit who had just been transferred to a "better" street crime detail working citywide. The anticrime officers were laughing about how this officer had been one of the least effective team members but noted that his next door neighbor is a good friend of the clerical man in the unit that he wanted to get into. Of course this story came from those left behind and was about someone who had found his way into a better assignment. In addition, we were told on several occasions by superior officers that cops are chronic complainers and always think the next guy has it better. Yet the belief persists almost universally among cops with whom we spoke that connections are "the only way to make it in this business."

With the exception of ethnic or racial joking patterns, we found little significant interethnic or racial tension or conflict in the social organization of either precinct. Groups of cops standing together for roll call or leaving the station house at the end of a tour would just as frequently as not be racially mixed. There were, however, very few self-selected radio car teams which were interracial in either precinct. Partnership in a radio car also helps to insure that officers leave work at the same time. Since black and Hispanic officers more often lived in the city while white officers commuted from the suburbs, they seldom shared a car pool and infrequently mixed socially outside of work. There was, however, some interracial and interethnic socializing outside of work in the Bronx precinct. There was an observable pattern of Hispanic and white officers socializing more commonly than black and white officers and black and Hispanic cops socializing more frequently than white and Hispanic cops.

There are task-related factors which seem to increase interracial mixing both at work and in social relations outside the job. In smaller working units such as anticrime or conditions units, social activities and parties usually included all members of the unit regardless of race or ethnicity. Generally, while cops seemed to restrict their socializing to "their own kind," the collective cop culture and the task organization seemed to be more effective than the divisive nature of ethnic or racial sorting.

A more complex picture emerges in the interaction between the police precinct in a minority community. In the Bronx precinct, for example, the population is of a lower socioeconomic class, predominantly Hispanic and, to a lesser extent, black. Most of the officers and virtually all of the bosses in the precinct are white. As mentioned earlier, the army of occupation character of their presence and the attitudes which they brought with them to the job are operative in creating mutual antagonisms. What seemed most important, however, was that we found very little evidence during interviews with community members, of any strong feeling that black or Hispanic cops or superior officers would provide better service or be any better received. Many of the people with whom I spoke, while pointing out that a Hispanic officer would at least be able to understand the language, insisted that "a cop is a cop" and did not see that color or language made much difference. In my experience, I saw an important difference between the handling of incidents or arrests on the street and the much more frequent job of rendering service or assistance in response to a complaint or emergency. The Bronx radio cars were most frequently dispatched to quell a family dispute or to take someone to a hospital because of the long delays experienced in awaiting an ambulance. I saw virtually no difference in the professional conduct of officers towards citizens between the Bronx precinct and the Manhattan precinct despite the great difference in the ethnic and socioeconomic status of the surrounding community.

Where street arrests were concerned, however, the distrust and suspicion of the white cops toward the black and Hispanic population was evident. Not only would a cop be more likely to view someone as being suspicious — such as someone walking down the street carrying a television set — in the Bronx, but they were also more concerned with the potential reaction of community members to an arrest than was true in Manhattan. This attitude, however, seemed no different among the black and Hispanic officers than the white officers in the Bronx. Here again it seems that the interface between the job of policing and the characteristics, real or perceived, of the surrounding community are most important. Many of the black and Hispanic officers said openly that they were "cops first," concerned with their careers and interested in transferring out of the precinct and into better assignments rather than with any sense of staying behind to police co-ethnics. When the department offered Spanish language training to Hispanic officers, many of the Hispanic cops we knew in the Bronx precinct steered clear of such specialization since, as one of them said, "I don't want to get stuck in a shit house my whole career just because I'm Puerto Rican and that happens to be the kind of precinct most Puerto Ricans live in now." Another Hispanic cop whose appearance and surname permitted him to be taken as Italian, commented, "It's worse out there for me if the people think I am one of them . . . then I'm supposed to give them the benefit of the doubt . . . but it never seems to work the other way, if I need their help . . . they still can't see beyond my uniform." Occasionally I heard antagonism toward co-ethnics such as, "Hell, I got a job, I'm not like them even though I started out with the same strikes against me, and I don't want them to think that I am like one of them."

While there were only a few hundred female officers in the New York City Police Department at the time of the study, and none were permanently assigned to either of the precincts under study, one group of female officers did come into the Bronx precinct for three months as part of a program for reintegrating rehired officers. There were some immediate problems such as having to set up separate locker and toilet facilities for the "girls." Possibly because everyone knew that this was not a permanent assignment, there was not much antagonism exhibited towards the policewomen but some of the antifeminist aspects of cop culture which I had observed in an earlier study emerged. There was joking about guys riding with one or two of the more attractive females, especially on the late tour, but the most frequent comments were, "They have to be kidding, expecting us to ride with girls in a place like this," or "They should be home having babies," and "A mother shouldn't be carrying a gun." There were frequent allusions to fooling around with the "girls" and this was accentuated because one of the policewomen had married a cop she had worked with in a former precinct. Both officers had been married before they met and both divorced their respective mates to marry each other. Comments on the topic of how and where they "got together" were not subtle or quiet. On the other hand, one female in the Bronx precinct was relatively well accepted by the men, to the point where several men did not object too strenuously to working with her. She was quite small and by no means the most attractive female in the group. What she did have was a quick-witted reparteé that is a cop's stock-in-trade perfected over long, often uneventful hours of riding with a partner. She was also quite bright and it seemed that she had somehow decided that the way to play the game was to become one of the boys. In so doing she found some measure of success, certainly more than the other female officers there at the time. Generally, the issue of female officers is one on which most police officers were in agreement — they could not be depended on because they were women.

Female officers, at least those who want to be on the streets in uniform and believe that they can handle the job as well as any man, complain that the real problem is in the men's head — in old-fashihoned, traditional notions and stereotypes of female characteristics and abilities. One female officer told about working a foot post when truckers began setting up picket lines. She reported this to the station house supervisor and asked them to send out barricades. The CO responded by sending out a lieutenant and four male officers with the barricades. She was told to return to the station house. She stormed into the CO's office demanding to know why she had been taken off post. He replied that he did not want to endanger her and that he was afraid that if the strikers started heckling her, the male officers would feel they had to come to her defense and that might escalate the situation possibly to the danger point. She said she was angry and frustrated at this put-down. "The guys blame us because they think they will get involved with us sexually if we are partners, or that it will give them trouble at home with their wives, not really so much that physically we won't be able to back them up. They are blaming us for something that's in their own heads." Unfortunately, the occasional stories of female officers who did not stand up under certain situations — such as the female radio team that was said to have locked themselves in their radio car and phoned for a back up when a psycho approached them — become the measure of police woman performance and the example of why women "just can't do the job." Several of the men admitted to a similar fear as that expressed by an officer who said, "I have enough problems explaining what I am doing when I get home late. Having to explain a female partner would really make my home life hell."

I found most cops were generally willing to accept the use of female officers for work involving youth, sexual abuse cases, decoy operations, or clerical work. There continues to be debate over whether a female presence in uniform escalates or deescalates tense situations; whether males will back down in a confrontation with a female cop because "you don't push women around," or whether a male's pride will be hurt, especially in front of another man, if a female officer attempts to control him. A cop in the Bronx precinct responded to this by saying, "You think those animals out here, if they are cornered, are going to stop and say . . . gee, she's a lady. They don't treat their own women like that, and if they want to get away, they'll blow her away as quickly as one of us. Pity the poor guy that is her partner when a girl gets hurt out there. He won't be able to live it down with the guys. It's unfair for them to set us up like that."

Departmental insistence on unpopular issues such as minority recruitment, community relations, and women on patrol are invariably attributed to downtown's lack of understanding, lack of involvement, and distance from the real job and its pressures. One officer, commenting on what he and others considered the failure of the department to back up the precinct during the initial investigation and subsequent trial in the Kelly case, summed it up: "The real problem is that the bosses aren't cops anymore, they are looking above them to the politicians because that's where they see their future, not down here on the streets where the job is. Decisions aren't made based on what's best for policing or even on safety in the city, but on political considerations; that's why they are pushing recruitment of minorities . . . even if they have criminal records or are female or fags."

> *Control and Supervision:* Street cop culture interprets management instituted control and supervision as a lack of trust. Street cop culture sees supervision as a reciprocal relationship to be negotiated. Management cop culture expects supervisors to act on clearly defined rules and procedures.

The attitude of the precinct officers toward downtown management cop culture corresponds roughly to their general attitude toward bosses and supervisors. All other factors being equal, the greater the supervisory distance, both in rank and geography between the officer and the supervisor, the greater the feeling of distrust and alienation. While this is not uncommon in other organizations, there are some particularly difficult aspects of supervision here. The immediate supervisor in the Kelly incident was the patrol sergeant who was responsible during that tour for the area in which the event took place. Following the general rule just outlined, patrol sergeants are usually perceived as "closest and most likely to understand" by precinct cops. The reason is probably best summed up by the cop who commented about the role of the patrol sergeant: "His ass is in the sling with ours if there is trouble out there." There are organizational problems with the functioning and authority of the sergeant. Every sergeant is responsible for evaluating a specific group of officers although he may not consistently work with those men. This is due to the unionization process with separate unions for patrolmen (the PBA), sergeants (the Sergeants' Benevolent Association), lieutenants (the Lieutenants' Benevolent Association), detectives (the Detectives' Endowment Association) and captains and above (the Captains' Endowment Association). Since each union is individually responsible for labor negotiations involving its own clientele, the work hour and tour charts negotiated by the PBA for cops do not necessarily coincide with that negotiated by the SBA for sergeants. The unions have been criticized for looking out only for the interests of their membership, in some cases at the expense of the best interests of the organization as a whole. The department has long been aware of the problem of asking supervisors to evaluate men with whom they do not work on a regular basis, but to date it has been impossible to rationalize the tour of duty charts for different ranks.

The number of sergeants supervising patrol activity on a particular tour is a function of the total number of sergeants working at the time. If only two sergeants are working, they divide the precinct in half. If one is working, he is responsible for all patrol activity. The patrol sergeant is responsible for street level supervision of all patrol activity. This involves assuring that all officers are on their assigned foot posts, and monitoring and occasionally checking on how assignments or jobs are handled by the radio car team. In some cases, there are calls for service that a radio car cannot handle without a supervisor's presence, such as an incident in a licensed premise (i.e., a bar), a kidnapping, a missing child or any unusual occurrence. The patrol sergeant can make it rough during a particular tour for the men who are working that tour, but except in smaller details where he is directly responsible for a handful of men, he has little opportunity to reward good performance. On the other hand, those for whom he is responsible on a particular tour can make life difficult for him or make him look bad to his immediate supervisors. For this reason, a sergeant must play a juggling game which involves protecting himself while not earning the enmity of the men whom he must supervise and still depend on during any given tour (Rubinstein, 1973). This role ambiguity helps to explain the cops' definition of a good patrol sergeant as "a guy who leaves you alone until you ask for his help," and of a bad one as "one who is always breathing down your back, showing up at the scene and taking over for effect," or, "always looking to catch you up short." "It's okay if he looks for you once on a tour to give you a scratch [initial your memo book] but when you know he is out there looking for you . . . then that's out and out harassment . . . then they are treating you like school kids and they deserve it if you act like a school kid."

There are a number of ways to handle difficult sergeants. Officers can, for example, legitimately call the sergeant to respond on any assignment and keep him running from one end of the precinct to another. The sergeant's driver plays a key role in the game because frequently the cops rely on him to make certain that the sergeant isn't at the wrong place at the right time. One night while riding with a sergeant who was known to be "straight," a call came over on a burglary in progress. The sergeant told his driver to respond to that run because, he explained, he wanted to check on response time and see how much investigation would take place. Also, I suspect, because the team given the job were known as "jokers," and he expected to catch them fooling around. When we arrived at the location, the sergeant went into the building (which was abandoned and partially burned) and I remained outside with the driver and the officers in another radio car who had backed up on the run. The officers were laughing with the sergeant's driver because he had taken the long way around, giving the sector car enough time to get there. The sergeant's driver had been paying close attention to where the sector cars were. In this case it was lucky for the sector car team that he did, because they had been in another part of the precinct. The sergeant's driver had called into central that he would be responding on the call, so the assigned sector car knew that they had to get to their location quickly.

Another factor that cops said influences the complex relationship between a sergeant and his men is the relative youth of many sergeants. Years ago, they say, the sergeant was a "tough old-timer with lots of years on the books," and there was little question of social distance. "He was the boss, and if he said jump, you said how high." Today, with more frequent sergeants' exams and larger lists, the sergeant is often an age mate of the younger cops. There is still, however, the paramilitary censure of fraternization. In one of the precincts, a sergeant who happened to be on the precinct football team was reprimanded by the CO for getting "too chummy" with the cops. He was known to drink and socialize with them during off hours and was told this would weaken his authority.

"Cops on patrol have too much independence, that's why we need more supervisory control," is how one lieutenant explained the functiuon of the patrol sergeant. But while rank in a paramilitary command structure confers unquestioned authority, it does not also confer unquestioned obedience. Rather, reciprocity describes the limits of whatever power of control the sergeant can exert and selective enforcement of the volume (literally) of departmental rules and regulations is the basis of that reciprocity. Thus authority and effectiveness is derived from a system of personal relations between supervisor and supervised and the system is constantly in flux — open to change, reinterpretation, redefinition, and even whimsy. A sergeant must become familiar with the working styles of his men and then impose his own style. A sergeant probably knows more about his men than anyone else in the department and for this very reason he must constantly weigh his duty as a supervisor with his working relations with his men. In a very real sense he must balance his loyalties — to the chain of command and rank structure, and to the men.

When I asked sergeants what they saw as their greatest responsibility, the response usually began with, "Carrying out the orders of my commanding officer." As I probed for details and examples, however, it became apparent that the reality was much more complex. The sergeant usually made spur-of-the-moment decisions that reflected more on the personalities involved in an incident than any hard and fast supervisory priorities or procedures (Manning, 1977). Although, because of different working charts, the sergeant and the cops do not always work the same tours, it does not take very long for the sergeant (or for anyone new to the precinct) to discover who are the workers and who are the shirkers. The sergeant knows which officers he can "give a little on," because he can be sure that if trouble comes, they will take the brunt of it and not make him look bad. Similarly, the men are capable of doing much of their own supervision over their colleagues."If a guy or a team doesn't hold up their end, it just means extra work for the rest of us out there," one officer explained. He spoke during a tour when his team was working in a sector next to a team that was known to be lazy and prone to taking care of personal business while on duty. "It isn't the matter of making the command look bad," he went on to explain. "Most of us stopped caring about the job a long time ago. But it means extra work for us and if wind of this gets out, then the bosses will be breathing down all our backs." His partner explained, "All of us can have an off night, or problems at home that just slow us down. It's understandable because it can happen to any of us and probably has on several occasions, but these guys are just goof-offs." Asked if they had ever reported the irresponsible team, one officer said "No, we don't really have to, they get the message when no one backs them up or when the rest of us slow down in responding to our calls and they have to pick up the slack for us." Another cop said, "That's the sergeant's job, if he can't find the guys who aren't working, what's he earning his salary for anyway?"

Perhaps because of the higher risks of violence in the Bronx precinct, the threat of not backing up on certain runs seemed a more serious recourse than it would have been in the Manhattan precinct where such runs or situations were less frequent. In terms of such peer monitoring it was interesting that in the Manhattan precinct, during a discussion of the same topic, one of the officers said, "Don't let them fool you with this talk of cop loyalties to other cops; if you get one of these guys mad at you, they'd just as soon drop a letter on you, or let on to one of the bosses that they should keep an eye on you."

There was little sympathy among the men, during the trial, for the patrol sergeant, who, it was argued, should have kept the situation from escalating. There was real concern, however, for the commanding officer of the precinct and the effect this trial would have on his career. Although he had not been at the precinct when the incident had occurred, the feeling was that he might suffer for the much publicized "blood on the squad room floor" quote from the trial proceedings or just from adverse trial publicity. Comments such as, "Downtown is just concerned with the bad press and public image that this kind of a trial creates, not whether someone is hurt," were frequent. Some officers mentioned that if trouble was made for the "turnarounds" still at the precinct, then the captain would get blamed for not being able to control his men, especially, again, if any of it got to the press.

The confusion surrounding the verdict of the jury in the Kelly trial points up the glaring ambiguities inherent in the public definition or perception of the police role as well as in any commonly accepted standard of "good" or even "proper" police action. Kelly was indicted on charges of second degree murder and first degree manslaughter. In charging the jury, the judge said that two lesser charges could be considered. One was second degree manslaughter, carrying a maximum sentence of fifteen years in prison. The other was criminally negligent homicide which carries a maximum sentence of four years. The jury voted to find Kelly guilty of the less serious charge. The confusion was a result of the fact that although the homicide charge resulted in the lesser of the possible sentences, it was in fact still a charge of murder. The jurors maintained that they thought the charge of criminally negligent homicide was a lesser count of manslaughter while it was in fact a lesser count of murder. When the jurors realized this, they were dismayed because as the jury foreman said in his affidavit, "If we had known that the charge came under the heading of murder, I'm sure we would have rendered a different verdict. At no time during these deliberations did I think that he was guilty of any degree of murder." Both the judge and the assistant district attorney who tried the case argued that a mistrial would be inappropriate. When the judge pronounced sentence, Kelly said, "I'm guilty of nothing. I was a police officer of the city of New York performing my duty." The sentence imposed was an indeterminate term of up to four years. A spokesman for the police department said there would be no comment from Commissioner Codd, "because it's not our position to comment. A conviction speaks for itself."

Analysis of the Event

What the Kelly trial did was to disrupt the social organization of the precinct, threaten the traditional values or ways of doing things of the street cop culture and reaffirm to the cops that there was an opposing set of values and objectives within the organization. Headquarters had been able to disrupt the traditional loyalty system by turning cop against cop at the trial. Ultimately, this was taken to mean that the old values would not long survive; thus group identification suffered and police officers emphasized the increasing importance of individual, rather than group, goals. This, say the cops, happens over and over as downtown looks towards the political system and not to the old loyalties for its justification. In the old days when the cop culture was the departmental culture none of this would have happened, say the cops. Either the incident would have been taken care of in-house and would never have received such public attention or, if it had reached the press, a consistent story would have been told by all the officers involved, in order to protect Kelly and ultimately themselves.

While it sounds as if the officers are excusing cover-up tactics, they assign a different level of interpretation for such behavior. What they are describing is an organic, almost kinship-like, relationship which makes all cops brother officers, with all of the sense of dependent relationships that term implies. Being able to depend on a brother officer in operational situations fraught with real or perceived danger does not, we were told, require or allow stopping to think whether the officer in danger is in the right or in the wrong. "Things happen too fast out there and so you do for that guy what you would want him to do for you." As a result Kelly's reaction to the suspect's shooting through the door was taken by many cops to represent his loyalty to the protection of all cops. Unless everyone in the system insures that every potential cop killer knows that he will be dealt with summarily by the police, no officer is safe. This same ethic becomes generalized in the street cop culture to cover all incidents of real or perceived danger to fellow officers, whether it comes from criminals, the public, or the department.

This sense of interdependency serves to produce an organizational self-image which excludes anyone who is not a sworn member of the department. Part of what accounted for this differentiation included the risks and dangers perceived as part of the job that was not in the experience of non-cops. But other aspects of it had more to do with job conditions, such as irregular hours and days off, and the officers' authorization for the discretionary use of force. That discretionary power, symbolized by the gun and the shield, represented the department on the street in confrontation with crime and disorder. Not all officers are in jobs which involve those risks, but the ethic is supposed to include all cops.

Where does the police officer learn this view of the job of policing and the cop culture that surrounds it? We were told repeatedly that it does not happen in the police academy and that one cannot learn it from books or criminal justice courses. A cop learns it from his own street experience, as an apprentice to officers already on the job and from contact with a peer structure of working cops in a precinct. The lessons are constantly reinforced by the "war stories" and experiences of other officers and through the traditions of police practice which developed in these networks. As the officer is socialized into the precinct social structure and into one of its subunits, the job comes to be governed by a series of conventions or mutual understandings among the officers. Kelly violated those conventions by exposing himself and other officers to unnecessary risks by his "crazy" (nonconventional) behavior. Kelly had already been sorted and labeled as a maverick and so his behavior was not unexpected. In addition, the officers who testified against him violated those conventions by breaking the bonds of loyalty, secrecy, and mutual protection. Their behavior could not be explained within the context of the traditional cop culture and so they had to be viewed as under pressure from "outside" forces from downtown.

This describes a different, nonpeer structure which encompasses the power relationships or formal authority structure from headquarters. A structure that is perceived as nonsupportive and working within a very different frame of reference. Headquarters thus becomes interorganizationally segregated and its behavior must be explained by the fact that they do not accept the values of the street cop culture because it has assumed a different set of values. Since everyone at headquarters began as a cop, their defection must also be explained by self-interest or having forgotten or refused to remember the risks inherent in policing, and thereby the requirement of a system of mutual dependence. The fact that some headquarters level police officers were never actually on the street and were assigned clerical and other inside jobs directly from the academy adds to this rationalization which was widespread in both precincts.

Not only during the Kelly trial but throughout our experience in both precincts, we found compelling evidence that precinct level cops not only feel isolated from those working at headquarters or the borough level but feel that such officers, regardless of rank, work with entirely different and frequently antagonistic priorities. "Not only are they not really cops anymore, but," they said, "they spend more time policing us than they do policing the city." As former cops, the headquarters management cops know enough about cop culture to determine where the points of vulnerability and possible malfeasance occur. Each frame of reference is, in fact, known to the other, and quite possibly both are right about the other.

The distinction between the precinct street cop culture and the headquarters management cop culture is important to organizational planning. The two cultures no longer share a common vocabulary, a common set of work experiences; they increasingly have different objectives. The unifying ethic which promised that "the department took care of its own," which was the moral for so many of the stories that we heard about the good old days, is now reinterpreted as, "The brass takes care of itself." As a result, two important changes in the pattern of social relationships have developed in the precinct level street cop culture. On the one hand, the cops at the precinct seem increasingly to emphasize individual over organizational, or even reference group, ends. I heard many cops say during the time of the trial that you can trust your partner, some of the guys in your squad, and a few of the guys you've worked with for a long time, and that's it. Similarly they are saying that given this new job attitude their only responsibility is to themselves and their families. "I can't count on anyone else anymore, and that means no one should count on me either." The second point is that while there was considerable, almost ritualistic social ostracizing of the turnaround officers, there was also public as well as private sympathy expressed for them by the cops. They were concerned with preserving their pensions and their jobs and understandably had to give in to the threats against their security from downtown because, "That's what the job is becoming."

It is important to point out that there is no neat distinction between everyone in the precinct being part of a street cop culture and everyone at headquarters being part of a management cop culture. In our contacts at police headquarters we met a number of officers of all ranks who understood and appreciated the realities of both cultures. In the precincts, we also found that there were administrative officers who could function in both cultures as well as some who were said by the cops to be unable to ever function successfully out from behind their desks. At both headquarters and precinct levels there are informal communications structures which tie the two cultures together under certain circumstances. A cop or a supervisor at the precinct level will usually, when he needs some information from headquarters which is important to him, contact a former partner or academy classmate to obtain the necessary information or favor informally. Similarly, a headquarters based officer wanting to know what's happening in the field or needing some favor "out there" will activate his own informal communication network to obtain that information or favor in spite of formal communication channels.

In any management-worker relationship, an important force is the workers' union. Here again, the NYPD has certain unique characteristics which make classical labor-management principles uncertain. While the PBA is the chief bargaining agent for police officers, there are, as was pointed out earlier, similar organizations for sergeants, for lieutenants, and for captains and above. Each association has its own interests at heart, frequently in competition with the other organizations. While police officers are enjoined from striking by New York State's Taylor Law, which covers all municipal unions,officers have gone on "job actions" which have all the characteristics of a classical strike. Not only do the several superior officer organizations not go out on sympathy job actions in support of the officers, they are often put in the position of being used as strike breakers. In addition, the strength of the street cop culture is such that despite growing pressure for professional union leadership, the head of the PBA and his staff are all elected from among working cops. The point is not lost on management.

The Kelly case is also illustrative of the process of group identification or sorting which emerges in the precinct social organization. In a classical bureaucracy individuals and groups identify with the values of the total organization. Much of the organizational literature in recent years, however, indicates that the individual worker's identification is much more frequently with the smaller, more immediate, working group to which he is organically related. The literature on occupational culture also points to the varying group loyalties associated with subunits within an overall system and indicates how group values and behaviors within these subunits determine individual values and mold behavior. Within a precinct, there are a number of dimensions by which subunits are formed. The basic distinction is between those working on the street or outside the station house and those who are assigned inside jobs. Being inside has always been considered a plus and generally believed to require a "hook," or connection. Both outside patrol units and inside staff are further subdivided into units or squads. These divisions set up functional subunits which form the largest collective for immediate sorting and group identification within the precinct. Thus, an officer will identify himself as being in anticrime or community relations or in a particular squad. Within and among these units there are other dimensions of sorting such as academy class, length of service, time in the command or assignment, ethnicity, sex, and whether or not the cop is connected to some power base. It is this process of sorting which establishes the various networks within the precinct and which forms the behavioral units which socialize the newcomer into the precinct. All of these networks are loosely coupled into the precinct social organization and generally share an identification with the precinct and the street cop culture.

CHAPTER 5
A Police Suicide

The social organization of the Manhattan precinct did not differ significantly from that of the Bronx precinct and both shared the precinct street
cop culture and perspective. While the event took place in the Manhattan
precinct, it could just as easily have occurred in the Bronx or elsewhere in
the city. This chapter will continue to point up the different perspectives,
or the situational perspectives, of both street cop and management cop cultures as well as how each of the participants in this struggle for control is
not able, or able only in part, to evade the controls of the other. It also
shows how street cop culture can, to some extent, effectively sabotage
management cop culture. The story of this chapter concerns imposition of
conventional management controls, practices concerning "gift" taking and
its relation to corruption and the relevence of the department's integrity
system as viewed by the street cops. It also points to career path issues and
problems in a system where everyone at the lowest rank is a "cop," but not
everyone does the same job. The reactions at the precinct to the event also
served to organize a good deal of information on how the organizational
structure of policing produces stress, and how that stress is seen as a different problem by street and management cop culture.

One spring day in 1978, around noon, I learned that one of the officers in
the Manhattan precinct had just committed suicide. My first impression
was that the suicide had taken place in the station house. Since at that time
I was working downstairs in the complaint room, but on that day not
scheduled to be there until a later tour, I decided to go in to work earlier to
observe what I expected would be considerable activity at the precinct in
reaction to the suicide. When I walked into the precinct house, I was
surprised to find that the officers and civilians working downstairs were
talking and behaving as usual and that there seemed to be nothing unusual
going on anywhere in the building. At first I thought that no one must

know about the suicide, or that perhaps our information had been incorrect. I phoned my informant and was told that the suicide had occurred in another borough when the officer was off duty. The officer had killed himself after other officers had attempted to arrest him in connection with a departmental investigation into his involvement with certain illegal activities.

After more than two hours of waiting, watching, and listening to the various activities and conversations throughout the building, I asked an officer if he had heard anything about one of their officers committing suicide. His response was casual: "Sure, we heard about it early this morning. They came in to look in his locker, but I don't even know who the guy is." I indicated my surprise at the apparent lack of concern by him and the other precinct personnel. He replied, "Listen, it would be like my hearing about a cop at another precinct committing suicide. . . . It's too bad, but it's no big deal to me, *he's* the one who got himself jammed up." Throughout the rest of the tour, I spoke with officers and occasionally one came up and asked if I had heard what had happened. Almost unanimously, the officers said that they could not recall much about him, that he was a young guy who had not been there long. The only thing that several of the officers said they recalled was that he wore dark glasses, and some officers suggested that he had a drinking problem and used the glasses to hide red eyes. What was surprising throughout the observations and discussions surrounding this event was the decidedly casual, almost disinterested attitude on the part of most of the officers with whom I talked. This lack of interest on the part of the officers at the precinct toward this incident, explained by, "He wasn't really one of us," was striking, particularly when compared with an incident that occurred earlier in the year involving the on-duty killing of two officers from another precinct. In that case, the lack of comment was explained almost unanimously as a result of the incident being too close to the fear with which most officers live, especially those working in uniform or on the streets. As one officer explained it, "We have to remove ourselves from it and so in a sense act as though it didn't really happen." The reaction on the part of the precinct officers to the cop who committed suicide is similar to the incident involving Officer Kelly in the Bronx because both men were considered by other officers to be different for some reason, and so largely outside the "brotherhood."

The attitude toward a fellow officer which I experienced in this situation is in opposition to the literature on police culture which suggests that all cops are brothers and will invariably band together in mutual support. The image suggested in the literature is a true image, I believe, when viewed from outside the department. Within the department, the pattern is not so consistent. As one of the officers explained several days after the suicide, "Cops are very sensitive towards criticism by outsiders because they feel that anyone on the outside can't possibly understand the job, its pressures, or a cop's reactions and attitudes. There is almost a feeling that the worst cop is still 'closer' than a civilian." He went on, "For that reason, a cop will keep silent before he will criticize one of his own in front of an outsider." Another officer explained, "Cops are very suspicious. I know that's almost a caricature of what you would find in books on police, but those authors really mean suspicious of outsiders. Hell, cops are even more suspicious of each other. They are always looking out for the guy who acts a little different, more so in recent years because of field associates, but also because they just don't know where to place a guy who might . . . well, like to drink on his own — whereas a guy who drinks socially with the other guys is regular. Or a guy who is married and will still go bouncing after work is okay, but not the guy who is married and is living with another girl and tries to keep it quiet from the guys."

The question of whom cops trust is a complicated one. First of all, it is clear that they have to trust each other about a lot of different things, not just the business of being sure the other guy will back them up in a tight spot. It also has to do with the fact that everyone is getting away with a little something (certainly not a situation unique to policing) by taking advantage of their position. What does this have to do with trust? "Well, the other cops are likely to know these things about you and could do you harm. So if a guy keeps some things secret or doesn't give you anything like that on him because he's very straight, then that guy isn't trustworthy." This must be one of the reasons that newcomers into the system are not immediately accepted.

Career and Salary: Management cop culture is doing away with the old reward system and so the old rules for getting ahead do not work. Street cop culture has not accepted the new social, economic and political realities of the management cop culture, so it continues to interpret and challenge all changes as not in its best interests.

When officers spoke of the illegal activity for which this officer was being picked up, the discussion usually turned first to the topic of money. Generally, opinion was not in favor of this officer's supplementing his salary through illegal activities because, "He was a single guy. If he had been married with a couple of kids to support, it might have been different." Other officers mentioned that if he had been around in the old days it would have been difficult to make the transition from the extra money readily available then "on the side," to living on take-home pay. The suggestion was that his involvement might have been understandable then as a reaction to "less take home pay, since nobody considered the goodies extras but were what a guy depended on every two weeks."

On pay day, every other Thursday, there is always much talk about what one really takes home after deductions and there is much comparing of overtime earned for that period. While comparisons of overtime accrued through arrests and/or court appearances is the subject of much good natured joking and some less than good natured jealousy, it is usually not hostile. There is a feeling among the officers who work the streets that, "Anything extra you can get is okay because at least you are out there where you are more liable to get hurt or in trouble than the guy working at a desk job or downtown."

The good natured tone is completely gone, however, when the officers talk about the pay difference (approximately $2500.00 per year) between themselves and the police officers who have been awarded a gold shield as detective specialists. Whatever the original intention of confering gold shield status to an officer (police officers wear silver, or "white," shields) — and apparently it was to reward superior performance by uniformed officers, thus motivating them to remain in precinct assignments — the distinction today causes serious morale problems, divisive internal competition, and jealousy within the precinct. In both precincts the explanation and the reaction were essentially the same: "Downtown gave out gold shields to have a handy pool of strike breakers and to keep us cops divided." Another officer added in the same conversation, "Yep, divide and conquer. That includes the use of field associates." This notion of an intentional departmental system of keeping the police officers divided among themselves because the department fears any show of their united strength could be interpreted as paranoia on the officers' part (and is, by some superiors). However, it was a pervasive enough theme in conversations that it has to be considered in understanding an officer's perception of the job. It was occasionally mentioned in connection with the variety of details that "guys don't want to give up, cause they can work out of uniform, or work steady tours, with weekends off. So there is no way we can all unite even though it would give us much more power." Another officer laughed and added, "Hell, we could take over the city if we could just all get it together for once." He went on to say, "Any time anyone suggests that we unite on something like a strike or a demonstration or making a boss that's being a prick look bad, I suddenly find out how many guys have cripples[1] in their families."

Officers have also expressed similar problems with the PBA over the system of special details possible at the police officer level. They suggested that uniformed cops on the street "always get the raw deal in contract negotiations because there are more guys in the PBA that work inside or special details." "What do they care or know about our problems,"[2] was the rhetorical question posed.

When the gold shield was originally distributed, it was at the discretion of a precinct commanding officer as a reward for those police officers who were doing an outstanding job. The intention was that it would be rotated among officers as a detective specialist would move up the career path ladder and out of the precinct. Gold shields were assigned to all precincts and did not go with the individual once he left the precinct for another assignment or rank. According to the grapevine, the COs gave them to "pets," and to those officers who held precinct staff positions that were frequently looked down upon by the patrol force, such as community relations and crime prevention officers, or used them to honor "contracts." "These officers didn't do anything different after they got the shields than before they had been awarded to them, except they now get $2500.00 more a year for doing it," we were told repeatedly. Another group of officers receiving gold shields were designated field training officers with the responsibility for training rookies just out of the academy. For the past several years, however, because of the fiscal crisis in the city, there have been no new officers out of the academy. Thus, there is now a situation where, for example, two radio car partners may do the same job and work the same hours, yet one might have the gold shield as a designated field training specialist with the attendant increase in pay and status. Officers at both precincts do not believe that there was ever any standard established for awarding the shields. They believe that it was based solely on favoritism or contacts. Similarly, the impression is that once someone has the gold shield, no one will try to make him look bad, or take it away from him, since, "No one wants to take money out of another guy's pocket."

Another area of resentment regarding the shield is that the precinct investigating units (PIUs — detective squads working out of the precinct) usually have several white shield police officer investigators assigned to them. Therefore those officers are working with, and frequently on the same cases as, gold shield detectives. Yet in the same precinct there are gold shield detective specialist designation cops working at jobs that have nothing to do with investigations, such as community relations and crime prevention. This has caused serious morale problems in the detective squads where the explanation for the gold shield system is that "Murphy [former police commissioner Patrick V. Murphy] hated detectives and wanted to lower their prestige, so he created the gold shield detective specialists, or 'funny badges,' for cops."

At issue also is the reality that at a time of diminishing budgets, there are fewer and fewer career possibilities within the department leading to a higher salary. Even the controversial connection between an officer's arrest activity and overtime payments ("collars for dollars")[2] is losing its attractiveness as more efficient court processing systems eliminate much of the overtime that officers spend in that process. A question regularly heard as officers left the station house at the beginning of their tour was, "Who's looking?" (That is, who wants to make an arrest on this tour.) This became a more anxious question of "Who wants one?" asked by cops trying to "give away" an arrest to another radio car team or to anticrime officers. Increasingly I heard that in lieu of money made through overtime, cops were taking on full-time, off-duty jobs to supplement their take home pay. This meant that they were actively avoiding making arrests that might tie them up after work or on a day that was now committed to another job, or even leaving them too tired from the arrest-related overwork.

An alternative career path is opened by taking and passing examinations for promotion. This, because of the current fiscal situation in the city, has not really been a viable option from the vantage point of many of the officers with whom we spoke. There are officers (and I spoke with many of them) who enjoy being cops, enjoy a foot post or a radio car seat and even enjoy an established routine year after year working with the same guys in the same precinct. Over and over again, we heard officers lament the fact that in order to bring home more money, they would have to take an exam and become a supervisor. Officers frequently expressed the feeling that "Doing what I am doing now [uniformed radio patrol] and what I know I am good at is a dead end. There's nothing to be made in overtime anymore. The best I can hope for is a detail where my hours might be better and I can work out of uniform but it won't bring any more money home."

One officer in Manhattan added another note: "There won't be any raises for the next couple of years, no shields, and you are going to find more guys starting to go back to the old ways." This officer went on to say that several years ago he had made $25,000 during one year with overtime but, "Now when you make an arrest that involves overtime, they treat you like you are crooked to be doing it." He concluded with, "The hell with them. If they don't want arrests, I won't give it to them. I'll just get a job outside and make my money there." In the same vein, another officer commented:

> There's nothing in it for me to make arrests or show too much activity because it won't get me anywhere anyway. Passing exams is the only way to get anywhere in this job anymore. . . . Not like in the old days. In the old days you wanted to show activity, you wanted to get ahead because it meant you could get yourself into a good house [precinct], and being in a good house meant that it was a place where you could make extra bucks. Now it doesn't much matter where they send you, except you can still probably make a little better money in overtime in Manhattan, but that probably won't last for long.

A cop standing with the group commented, "But who wants to get their names on that list [which the department keeps of top overtime earners for the year]. They treat you like you're on the ten most wanted list. You get into trouble anyway if you make too much overtime, because the boss gets heat from the borough." "Don't make waves, that should be the motto of this job," another cop added. "If they notice you, no matter what the reason, good or bad, its got to be bad for you sooner or later. So your best bet is to just lay low, go about your business, don't bother anyone, put in your time and then get the hell out of the city."

A young cop in the Manhattan precinct noted, "Old timers didn't have the skills outside the job to turn to, so they kept quiet and kept working." He suggested that the younger officers coming into the department over the last ten years have more career potential and possibilities outside, and so "the department better watch out that it doesn't lose a lot of good, young officers because it doesn't have anything to offer them anymore." He went on, "For the old timers, this job is their only career, but I'm getting a degree in public administration and so I'll have something to turn to when I get out of here, or if things get too bad, I can just pack it in early."

> *Job Stress:* Management cop culture sees in job stress the potential for police action that can lead to public relations problems. The public needs to be protected from cops who are out of control. Street cop culture interprets stress as a very immediate, personal, and individual reaction to handling a difficult job. When an officer runs into problems because of stress, he needs to be protected.

The day after the suicide, a group of officers standing in the hall were discussing the possibility that the officer who had killed himself had a drinking problem. The topic became generalized to the problem of drinkers on the job and one of the officers commented, "If you are a drinker, they'll just steer clear of you as long as you don't step out of line too badly." Another officer suggested, "There must have been something else wrong with the guy for him to go off the deep end like that. He kept so much to himself. Only a few of the guys even recognized him. The worst that could have happened to him, even if the department had him on those charges, was that he would lose his pension and anyway, I don't think he had a family to support."

The NYPD has an alcoholism counseling section and a recently added departmental psychological services unit. Usually these services come into play only after the fact and frequently only after a very serious incident affecting the officer's performance on the job, or an injury to a citizen. The alcoholism counseling program has been under the control (many officers say "domination") of an Irish, Roman Catholic monsignor, who holds the honorary rank of inspector. Some officers who have been in his program describe him as more of an inspector in bearing and attitude than a priest-counselor. However, if we had not been aware of the existence of these units before the study, we would not have learned of their existence through discussions with precinct cops. There was never any reference to officers turning to such programs for help or advice on problems, although I was privy to many conversations on personal and job related problems. At one point in the study, I intentionally began asking about these units as resources available to the men, and found it difficult to get beyond some very pejorative, albeit colorful, language about their usefulness.

The dominant theme in discussions of these services was, "Don't get involved because if you do it will mark you for the rest of your career." I spoke with nine officers who had some extensive involvement with either alcoholism counseling or psychological services. Two officers had gone voluntarily, one to counseling and the other to the psychological services unit. The cop involved in alcoholism counseling felt that he had been helped considerably by going there and added that he had not had a drink since that time. He also said that he did not feel that his connection with that program had hurt, or would hurt, him in his career, but felt that it might jeopardize some career possibilities outside of this job if it were known that he had once had a drinking problem. "Hell," one officer said during a discussion, "drinking is an occupational hazard in this job and most of the guys, even the desk lieutenants, will cover for a guy who comes in a little under the weather on a tour. Anyway the 'Church' [the monsignor] still has a lot of pull with the top brass, although not so much as in the old days." Other officers have told us, "The same officers go back regularly to the farm to dry out." (The department runs a treatment facility outside of the city where officers go, or more frequently are sent, to dry out and get counseling services.) "The problem with them is they start preaching at you about the evils of drinking and can really drive you nuts with their superior attitude."

The reaction of the seven officers who had been sent by the department to psychological services was unanimously hostile. All of these officers had subsequently been placed on restricted duty and all had elaborate stories to tell of how "the job screwed them." In three of the cases, marital problems had deteriorated to such a point that the officers had threatened their wives with guns. In these cases, the wives had called the department and reported their husbands. In another case, the officer had voluntarily turned in his guns because, he told me, "I was afraid that I couldn't control myself and the damn gun is so convenient." This particular officer had been on restricted duty for over a year, had subsequently been divorced from his wife and was living with a girlfriend. He wanted his gun back and wanted to be put on regular duty again.[3] This officer told me that he had even paid for his own psychiatrist who had several months earlier written a letter to the department saying that in his professional estimation this officer was fit to be returned to full duty. But time had passed and nothing had happened and the officer was getting more and more frustrated. He said that he intended shortly to get a lawyer and put in for "three-quarters" (medical disability pension), arguing that if the department did not think he was fit to perform active duty, then they were saying that he was psychologically disabled, so he should be pensioned out on a disability. He added, "And I wouldn't have any trouble proving that it was job related." One afternoon, when I stopped to ask him if he had heard anything about his situation, he laughed and said that he had some luck. It seems that he had heard informally from downtown that they were going to move on his case. However, shortly after this, he said, an article in the newspaper reported that a police officer on restricted duty had been recently reassigned on his psychiatrist's advice. He had been given back his guns and a few days later had shot his neighbor during a quarrel. The officer shrugged his shoulders and said that this would put his case back six months, because, "There is *no way* this department is going to take a chance on looking bad. They could give a shit about me or any guy and his own problems. They are going to protect themselves."

The other problem mentioned simultaneously in this context is that although the department maintains that referrals to alcoholism and psychiatric units are kept confidential, no one believes it. Several officers have told me stories of cops who went to apply to other places for jobs and "somehow the new job finds out that we have been to 'psych' services and that kills it." For the cop, this means a breach of trust and is one more indication that headquarters does not care about cops as individuals. The response from the bosses is usually, "cops are chronic complainers and paranoid about everything."

> *Integrity and Ethics:* Management cop culture has imposed department-wide techniques and practices for controlling activities by officers that are not in keeping with departmental rules and procedures. Street cop culture views these techniques as part of the game and officers devise ways of beating the system.

The officer who committed suicide was under departmental investigations for illegal activity. Many cops told me that a cop who gets involved in making money illegally usually does so because he cannot pay his bills. I came to realize that the reference to "the old days" which prefaced many such discussions was not a generalized nostalgia for the past, but referred to a specific point in time. The old days, when I heard it used in this context, meant very specifically the days before the Knapp Commission investigation into police corruption. A majority of the officers with whom I spoke, including officers of supervisory rank, felt that much of the current organization and practice in the department was designed in reaction to the commission's findings on types of corrupt activity and policing conditions particularly conducive to corruption. Many of the cops I talked to in both precincts commented that "the cure was worse than the sickness." A typical comment of an officer who had been on the job long before the Knapp Commission was, "What has changed this job for the worse is a result of the bosses and downtown being scared shitless of us being caught off base. . . . The problem is that *they* made the new rules and *we* have to live with them."

Since the Knapp Commission, the department has adopted an integrity program, the Ethical Awareness Workshops, which run in cycles throughout the year and which all officers are expected to attend. Workshops are run by police officers assigned to that unit. Outsiders are strictly forbidden to attend since the officers who run the program want the officers attending the workshop to feel completely free and confident to discuss their problems and air their complaints. A weekly summary of general areas of discussion and issues arising in the sessions is passed up through the system to higher ranking officers for their information. While a few officers claimed that the sessions are monitored to collect information to use against the cops, the vast majority view it simply as "R and R" (rest and recuperation). One cop added, "So it lets the bosses downtown think they know something about what is going on out in the streets." More vehemence could be detected, however, whenever officers talked about the final day of the three-day cycle, when the program calls for a ranking officer to be present "to field any questions that the officers might have on issues that came up during the other days of the workshop." "What kind of fools do they take us for?" one officer complained. "It's a lot of crap having one of the bosses stand in front of us and talk about integrity. Who are they trying to fool? They were there when the money was changing hands, only the system has changed, so its to their advantage to keep their hands in their pockets now. But we're still out there. Why do they expect us to be any different than they were?" Another officer suggested, "Who are they trying to kid? All of a sudden they're so clean? They were in it up to their necks. How else do you think they know where to look for us and what to look for? Because they were doing the same things. Why do you think they have tightened up so much on us? Because they know how easy it is out there."

In both precincts it was apparent from observation and interviews that it is still possible for an officer or a team to become involved in activities generically referred to as "corrupt practices." What the department has managed to do, however, is to make organized corruption very difficult and, more importantly, to make institutionalized corruption even less likely. The officer who committed suicide, as well as others who were charged with corruption or illegal activities, acted as individuals. This does not mean that the amount of corruption or illegal activity has decreased significantly but rather that systematic corruption is no longer supported by the system. In 1979, for example, it was reported that there had been significant increases in the number of complaints of corruption against police officers. A police department spokesman said that this could be the result of better detection or could represent an actual increase, but probably was a result of a greater willingness on the part of civilians as well as cops to turn in cops. Similarly, in the years following the Knapp Commission report, there was a significant decrease in the number of complaints against officers for taking bribes related to gambling, which was a highly organized form of graft. But there was an equally significant increase in the number of officers reported as being involved in a more individually oriented taking of bribes from narcotics sources.

I never observed instances of such conduct on the part of officers at either precinct. I did observe (and I feel that the openness with which it was done in my presence attests to the informal level of acceptance of such practices) with some frequency activities that might more appropriately be referred to as infractions of departmental rules and procedures, or "stealing department time." This includes such activities as taking care of personal shopping or personal business during working hours, stopping in at a social club, bar, or restaurant for a free drink, a free meal, or discounts on items. While I found little difference between the two precincts in terms of frequency or type of activity involved, what seemed to make the difference in the two precincts was what was available in the different communities. A girlfriend in the Bronx might be a local girl working in one of the clubs, while in Manhattan she might be an airline stewardess. "Stopping in for a drink" in the Bronx might mean dropping by a neighborhood social club, while in Manhattan it might mean a French restaurant shortly before opening. "Discount shopping" in the Bronx might mean a better price on a car battery or free fruit from the Bronx Terminal Market at 4 a.m. in the morning; in Manhattan it could be a special price on an imported leather coat.

There is sufficient secrecy displayed in many of these activities to indicate that the officers do feel a degree of caution because someone may be watching. This caution, however, has a gaming quality to it. Almost immediately after turning out for the tour, the first question asked, even before "Where shall we go for coffee?" is, "Who's got the desk?" Cops are very conscious of which bosses are working, or if "the old man [the CO] is in." Extra precautions can also be taken to virtually insure safety, unless, as is frequently suggested, "They are out to get us," in which case, "There is no way we're going to [i.e., can] hide." In one case, I was riding with a radio

car team at night. The team stopped in for a lengthy drink and some socializing in a bar. To cover themselves in case anyone was watching they put in
a "pick-up" (an incident observed as the radio car is cruising along the
streets, rather than being assigned to them over the car radio) on a "dispute in progress," and so logged themselves into the central dispatch system as "out," handling a legitimate incident. Usually, word will get out at
the precinct if someone from IAD is watching the precinct, or "sitting on"
a particular spot such as a social club frequented by the officers from that
precinct. We had, of course, no way of verifying how correct such rumors
were, but they occurred with some frequency, adding somewhat to the
risks of the game.

In general, the officers with whom I spoke seemed to feel that the department's public and vocal preoccupation with integrity and corruption
was essentially a "kneejerk" reaction which increased following any media
attention or widely publicized scandal, and then simmered down. Most frequently, it was described as a "cover your ass" response where, as long as
you are quiet and relatively circumspect about your "personal business,"
you are not likely to get into trouble. When, however, the department
needs to offer up "a victim, because the papers or city hall are howling for
somebody's blood, then watch out, there's nowhere to hide."

Analysis of the Event

Although I was in the Manhattan precinct for only one-third of the
amount of time spent in the Bronx, familiarity with precinct level activity
gained in the Bronx made both my introduction into the precinct and my
understanding of its social organization much easier. In fact, some of the
cops I worked with in the Bronx informally contacted officers in the Manhattan precinct to vouch for me, making my *entré* much easier. I had been
told in the Bronx and by some police administrators with whom I discussed
the choice of the Manhattan precinct that the two precincts would be "as
different as night and day." I found, however, that the universality of
street cop culture at the precinct level was such that while there were some
differences between the two precincts, they were more in form than in
substance. There was more emphasis on personal appearance and proper
uniform attire in Manhattan where, for example, I observed that officers
almost always followed department regulations and put their hats on when
leaving their radio cars. Cops in both precincts explained this difference by
the fact that, "In an active precinct you don't have time to worry about
your hat and the bosses are more concerned with response time than they
are with what you look like when you get there." Or, "Since the bosses are
always looking to catch you up short, they can get you in the Bronx for
slowing down on the job but in Manhattan where there is so little real ac-

tivity, they go after you on anything they can." I had been prepared by the Bronx cops for a "quiet, spit-and-polish" house in Manhattan where the guys "don't do anything but cruise around those clean streets looking at girls." I found, in fact, that the station house was just as physically run-down as the one in the Bronx and that the sector cars seemed almost as busy as in the Bronx, at least in number of runs. However, by and large the radio runs were less frequently for violent activities and in a surprising number of cases were unfounded burglar alarms.

The characteristics of the area also made for differences in the sense of territoriality which integrated police officers into the community. The hospitality of the surrounding area provided more and better opportunities for "discount shopping" and for gratuitous meals and drinks. There is also a different view of social distance here where the rich and powerful live as contrasted to the poverty level areas of the Bronx precinct. However, the cops apparently feel just as alienated from the community here as they do in the Bronx, but for different reasons: "They treat us like servants or like we aren't even there. Businessmen don't like us around where people can see us when we have to take reports on a burglary or a hold-up because they think it discourages customers." There also seem to be more individualism and less close social bonding here than in the Bronx, where the station house offered a place of refuge from a hostile environment. A cop who had worked in both boroughs in similar types of precincts summed it up: "In Manhattan they don't say thank you officer because they think they are too good for you; in the Bronx they don't say thank you either, but there they might curse at you as well. It's all the same to me, I do my job and treat them both the same."

The role of the internal affairs division (IAD) in the investigation leading to the suicide was frequently cited by cops who were quite outspoken about this kind of activity as being just another proof that management cop culture is out to get them. The cops agree that IAD has a legitimate role in ferreting out corruption but they also believe that they go about it the wrong way. Since IAD is viewed in the precincts as part of "downtown" and responsive to management cop culture, the feeling is that they have to "get on the sheet, too" and produce results for their bosses regardless of what it does to individual lives or careers. Further, IAD uses field associates, who the men believe are for the most part cops who have gotten into trouble and so are susceptible to being pressured into spying on their fellow officers in order to escape punishment for their own misdeeds. The fact that the cops know that some field associates went straight into those assignments from the academy does not ease the bitterness, since the perception here is that anybody who accepts a job "ratting" on brother officers has to be a maverick. It is not, say the cops, that they believe that wrongdoing should go unpunished, but rather that the matter should be turned over to the precinct commander so that the social control system within the precinct can deal with the situation. Instead, the information is sent downtown, often with the commanding officer being unaware of the investigation and like the cops, "reading about it in the *Daily News* along with everybody else."[4]

Considered together with the case of Officer Kelly, the events surrounding the suicide point to one major consequence of the increasing separation and conflict inherent in the two-culture organizational structure. The seeming disinterest on the part of Manhattan precinct officers over the troubles and subsequent suicide of a brother officer is an example of what the cops mean when they say that "downtown wants us to not trust the other guy." Just as officers were willing to testify against Kelly in the Bronx precinct, so officers here indicated little active concern and were quick to note that "we hardly knew him." Both Kelly and the officer who committed suicide were described as "mavericks," guys relatively new to the precinct who had not yet been accepted into the precinct social organization. While Kelly was better known in the Bronx precinct than the officer who committed suicide was in the Manhattan precinct, both were described as deviant from the cop norm in some fashion. Kelly was a "crazy" who was known to be unpredictable and prone to violence and drinking, while the officer who committed suicide was described as a "loner" who just did not fit in with any of the established social networks in the precinct. In the good old days this would not have mattered and the protective web of relationships would have reached out to embrace them as well because downtown was looking out for every cop. What the cops are suggesting is that in the old days the game was to cover the individual officer because he was part of the system. Today the new game is to find some way to identify him early and get him out quickly.

Since the Knapp Commission investigations there has been a great deal of attention and department time spent on the design, development, and implementation of integrity and ethical awareness programs. In both precincts, most of the officers did not feel any ownership or real involvement with these programs, but spoke of them as a joke. Their view was that the programs had been developed and carried out by management at headquarters in response to external pressures and for political expediency, and the pressure came from people who know virtually nothing about the problems of the street cop. At the same time that they complain about this lack of awareness, however, the street cops also maintain that these same officers and bosses who are pushing these programs were part of the good old days when not only free meals, but institutionalized payoffs, were accepted, and that even if they were not personally involved, they were part of the system and "weren't blowing the whistle on anybody." There is also a sense that cops are being singled out unfairly in a societal milieu where favors and gifts are not unknown in business, industry, and government. One story I heard on several occasions was used to illustrate the point. It seems that a police officer was invited to lunch by lawyers from the Knapp Commission and questioned on how widespread the practice of accepting free lunches was in his precinct. The meal was paid for on the lawyers' expense account.

Integrity programs are viewed as an imposed ethic from downtown, which has little or no meaning in the social and work context of the precinct. Even the new integrity and ethics workshops which officers are required to attend are viewed suspiciously as a mechanism by which individual officers will be pressured into turning in fellow officers or reporting on new "scams." Our impression was that as a management technique for gathering information on "the troops," or even as a control device, they are of minimal value.

While the department has been successful in eliminating large-scale systemwide organized "pads,"[5] it has been less successful in combating institutionalized but individualized problems with integrity. There is considerable stealing of department time by officers, as well as "discount shopping" and free meals in much the same way that a worker will get as much as he can from a large anonymous corporate employer. In fact, some cops become minor culture heros to their peers because of the impunity with which they work the system to their advantage, without getting caught.

Despite the apparent disinterest in the officer who committed suicide, there were a number of comments which, while they did not condone his illegal activity, did express understanding of his looking for opportunities to earn extra money. The rationale here suggests that since there is little chance of vertical movement or substantial salary increases in the department, cops are increasingly looking to moonlighting in other jobs during off-duty hours in order to make ends meet. Here again, the educational programs designed to improve police performance are said to instead provide better competing career opportunities. A number of officers indicated that they were more committed to their outside jobs since they saw them as eventually leading someplace.

One of the most frequently cited examples of how the new politics has changed the police career is described in the attitude towards the gold shield. On numerous occasions I was told that some officer, in the estimation of his peers, should have been awarded the gold shield because of his performance. Instead, they complain, gold shields have to be parceled out to blacks, Hispanics, and women, as well as to people who are well connected. One cop added, "I guess they are going to have to save some for the fags when they are officially welcomed in." The cop culture's humorous view of life in "cushy" details indicates the envy and the tension within the street cop. In the lampoon issue of the police magazine *Spring 3100*, head-quarters details, detective specialist designations, and civilians are ridiculed in a humorous anecdote entitled, "No Soft Detail."

> A tough day at 1 Police Plaza occurred recently that illustrates the hazards of non-patrol duties. It began when Det. Specialist Alan Whock caught his tie in his model 5000 Electric Wizard typewriter. As the beserk machine rolled up his tie and drew Whock into its clutches, the specialist managed to cut his tie off (he had already been struck in the face by several capital letters) before losing consciousness. As he jumped back, however, he inadvertently tipped over a 32 pot coffee urn which hit two civilian employees and began dissolving the accumulated wax on the office floor. Attracted by the screams of the scalded civilians, Chief of Borough Reconnaisance Ernest Qualm stepped from his office. In an attempt to guard his leader from slipping in the coffee-wax mixture, Det. Whock launched himself at the Chief. As the two tumbled across desks they dislodged several lamps whose exposed wires made contact with the liquid, shorting out the Headquarters complex and leaving 911 out of service for 9½ hours. Fortunately, the only permanent damage was to the office spider plant which suffered severe trauma due to the shouting and screaming. It has since perished.

One of the major results of the loss of a unifying culture in the department is the increasing evidence of organizational stress which affects police behavior. Police work has always been considered a high stress occupation with factors such as danger, violence, and erratic working hours causing serious problems for health and effectiveness. The old ethos demanded that the major symptoms of stress, drinking and marital problems, be kept inside the department, and the officer was protected by being given some nonsensitive assignment until he straightened out or retired. Today, say the cops, those jobs are held by civilians and the management culture is more interested in the early identification and weeding out of potentially embarrassing officers then in protecting one of their own.

As the unifying culture dissolves and the two cultures are increasingly in conflict, there are also organizational control and role pressures which add to that stress load, often at an unconscious level, for both the individual and the organization. Today, the NYPD has many of the organizational stress characteristics of any city agency in a time of financial crisis but there are some which are peculiar to the police function. Organizations provide a behavioral home for the people who work in them, shaping their self-images, their career goals and aspirations, their work and how it is organized, and other factors which affect the constructive or destructive results of stress. Organizations also can become stress *provoking* when some significant segment feels manipulated by forces beyond its control, or by contradictory goals, or when it thinks that its work role or status is demeaning or has been demeaned by others.

Organizationally generated stress is increased when some group or groups feel that they are being pitted against each other or that some members of the organization are spying on others. Even promotional and reward systems can be stress producing. The gold shield designation among police officers inevitably means that for each person promoted or rewarded a number are left behind or ignored. This presents a particular problem among police, where the selection and training process and the close bonds among officers produces a cohort system against which one can measure one's progress. This can, however, add to feelings of alienation from the group, depression, and lowered self-esteem when one is passed over. Finally, there is the problem of the management of stress. Frequently, people in any kind of work that requires face-to-face contact with troublesome or irate clients have difficulty managing their own hostile reactions. Policemen have this frequent provocation to anger and aggression complicated by the added stress of continuous exposure to real and perceived danger as a constant aspect of their job. All of this is made more complex by the policeman's discretionary authority to use force. It is this latter threat which is most disturbing to police management and the recent escalation of interest on stress in police work by the department is largely oriented towards identifying and neutralizing potentially violent officers who might become dangerous to others when under stress. Here again, the precinct cop sees a self-serving management culture which is more interested in avoiding the public and political repercussions of an incident than they are in organizing police work to reduce dysfunctional organizational stress.

Notes

1. The tongue in cheek implication here is that there are special extenuating circumstances, e.g., that someone in the family is crippled, and that not just his own personal comfort is at stake.
2. If a police officer makes an arrest he must take the prisoner through a lengthy arrest and booking process. If the arrest takes place close to the end of his tour of duty, the extra time needed for this process would lead to overtime hours and this means extra pay for the officer making the arrest. It has been suggested that, not infrequently, officers would deliberately make arrests at the end of the tour in order to make overtime money.
3. The importance of the gun as a symbol of the officer's authority is evident when restricted duty cops are referred to as being assigned to the "bow and arrow" or "rubber gun" squad. During 1977, about 100 officers, we were told, were forced to work without guns on nonpatrol assignments. Their weapons were removed because they were found to be suffering from psychiatric problems and considered potentially dangerous. These officers were identified through an "early warning system" used to seek out violence prone or unstable officers. Since 1973, when the system was instituted in the department, records of poor performance or seemingly abnormal behavior are reevaluated and officers who are suspected of having difficulties are referred to psychological services.

Commanding officers may refer officers to the psychiatrist for a variety of reasons, such as chronic sickness, disciplinary problems, alcoholism, or frequent civilian complaints or charges of brutality.

4. Several months after I left the precinct, newspaper accounts reported that there had been at least one field associate present in this precinct. As a result of information he supplied, a number of cops were disciplined by headquarters for not responding to radio calls, drinking while on duty, and accepting free meals from local restaurants. The commanding officer was transferred.

5. The "pad" is a police slang term and refers to regular weekly, biweekly or monthly payments, usually picked up by a police bagman and divided among fellow officers. Those who make such payments as well as policemen who receive them are referred to as being "on the pad." From: *The Knapp Commission Report on Police Corruption* (N.Y.: George Braziller, 1973).

CHAPTER 6

A Management-by-Objectives Plan and the Citywide Blackout

Two additional events helped us organize our data on social organization at the precinct level and also added some important insights into how street cop culture actually organizes the job of policing and the code of rules which enpowers it. The first was an attempt on the part of the management cop culture at headquarters to implement a management-by-objectives (MBO) program throughout the department. The program came from outside the department as the city administration instituted such programs in all city agencies as part of a master plan for increasing productivity and accountability. I was at the precinct when the memorandum mandating the program was first issued and was able to follow it through to its demise. In addition, I was able to study it through the next command level, the borough, since I was permitted to attend several planning meetings. While I could not follow it up to headquarters with the same degree of detail as I had at lower levels, I did discuss its intended and actual consequences with a number of ranking management and planning officers.

Shortly before the issuance of the memo implementing the MBO program, a dramatic and unexpected event took place which permitted the observation of crisis response at the local level, management planning for emergencies and its "fit" with precinct response. In July, 1977, there was an electrical blackout in New York City, which lead to widespread looting and destruction of property in the Bronx precinct and throughout the city. I was present at the precinct during the blackout and observed decision making processes and resultant activity at the local level. I was also able to obtain information on what precinct level personnel understood that headquarters wanted in handling this crises. Because the events took place within the same general time period and since they rather nicely illustrate an unexpected crisis and precinct response, in contrast to a rationally designed planning program and precinct response to it, the two events will be described and analyzed together.

In describing both events, I have once again been faithful to the observations and interviews which grew out of the patterns of activity generated by these events. I have also included information which goes somewhat beyond the events to describe additional aspects of precinct social organization and street cop culture which give it meaning. Considered together, the events are yet another example of the street cop's perception of the management cops as allies of the political system. Divorced from the street, they are involved in making political rather than policing decisions. They also illustrate the conflict inherent in the necessity for choosing between administrative process and service delivery. There are a number of other organizational points exemplified by these two events. One is an apt demonstration of what takes place when authority and responsibility are not coincident in the same roles. They also illustrate the importance of understanding police work as what cops actually do rather than what they say they do or what a distanced administrative structure believes they should be doing.

It is important to point out the constraints that the organizational structure of the department places on various work functions within the precinct and some of the maneuvering and adjusting which cops resort to when they feel the need to rationalize departmental policies to fit local conditions. The coexistence of formal and informal rules and conventions which establish behavioral limits tells the members of the precinct what they can and cannot get away with, depending on who is in charge at the time and what are the immediate environmental pressures. Finally, particularly in the case of the blackout, we have a vivid demonstration of what happens in police work when there is conflict in goals, missions, and expectations between workers and managers. The conflict between the two cultures makes it impossible to act effectively from almost any point of view.

Management-by-Objectives Plan

In November, 1977, a departmental memo came down to all area and specialized unit commanders from the chief of field services. The memo outlined the Field Services Agency Plan Supplement which was intended to implement a management plan concept mandated for all city agencies by the new mayor. The memo called for the various departmental units, including precincts, to "develop specific objectives or standards within which to measure command performance in priority areas of concern." While the memo indicated that the development of objectives and standards was the responsibility of each command, it contained a "Management Improvement Program Format (which is helpful in establishing programs with specific objectives, milestones, and delineation of responsibility) designed to assist a command in reaching its management plan objectives or in achieving improvement in a separate area of command concern through the conduct of specifically programmed activities."

When the commanding officer of the Bronx precinct told me about this order, he suggested that it might be a good opportunity to study the impact of departmental planning and decision making on precinct level operations. Compliance with this order, he indicated, would necessitate a thorough evaluation and analysis of current precinct activity with projections for future activity. It would also involve several meetings of precinct-based units in order to get the input of those officers responsible for meeting that objective. Most interesting for my purposes, however, would be the testing of a basic principal of public administration: policy made at the higher levels of an organization will be effective only if each successive lower level complies with that policy and/or is capable of carrying it out. It was our impression from previous experience with the department that if an administrative order does not obtain the cooperation of the patrol force it cannot succeed. And further, that the patrol force will understand and interpret any such order not in terms of some generalized departmental goals or policies, but rather in terms of their social environment and particularly in terms of the anticipated or perceived reactions of fellow officers who constitute their immediate reference or work group.

While each command was to establish its own objectives there were broad objectives established on a department-wide basis and these were defined in the memo as:

> Bureau-wide priority objectives related to reducing and controlling serious crime, increasing community involvement in crime prevention and other programs, improving police-community relations, reducing administrative costs and maintaining the climate of integrity at a high level. When the [Area and Special Command level] objectives are developed, Field Services Bureau will have at every level of command, standards against which progress and accomplishment may be measured in reference to Bureau-wide priorities.

Attached to the memo was a listing of the responsibilities for various command levels and charts listing a series of performance indicators for the various priority areas. Objectives were established by estimating (on a quarterly basis) the number of complaints for burglary, for example, which would be reported in the next year in comparison to the number reported the previous year, and a precinct's performance would then be measured by comparing the actual number of complaints reported with what had been projected.

The commanding officer delegated responsibility for setting up the new program to a lieutenant who had once been assigned to a planning and evaluation unit. The previous year this lieutenant had attended a three-day course on planning and evaluation offered to all sergeants and lieutenants by the American Management Association. The planning process described in that course, the lieutenant told me, was very similar to that outlined in the memo and differed only in terminology. He had called over to the borough command office when he was given this assignment and asked if it would be possible to set up a refresher course since he did not see how any of the precinct personnel assigned to carry out the planning process outlined in the memo could handle it without special instruction. The borough command's response was, "Handle it as best you can." This, he suggested, reinforced his opinion that since a new police commissioner was going to take over in the next few months, the new plan probably would not survive beyond the change in administration. When he called the field services bureau to clarify some other specifics of the plan, he was told not to worry about it since precinct commanding officers would not be held accountable for the success of the plan and would not be evaluated on its outcome. This conversation, he said, convinced him that they were all involved in another exercise in futility. It was seen as just another example of "downtown coming up with another way to keep the guys in the field busy and at the same time justify their own existence."

> *The Numbers Game:* No one has developed a system of measuring the quality of police activity. What is measured is what is most easily measured. Management cop culture has to produce numbers to prove its accomplishments. The street cop does not see how any of it helps him do his job.

The lieutenant pointed out that one immediate problem with complying with the request was that "they were asking for numbers, exact figures, not even ratios." They were back to playing "the same old numbers game," where precincts in each borough are in competition to place first, second, third, etc. He shook his head and pointed out that, although all the recent literature in management indicates that numbers are not a reliable measure of performance, the system keeps justifying and accounting for activity on the basis of more numbers.

A compounding problem in responding to this request was the fact that on January 3, 1978, all precincts in the Bronx would be changing their boundaries to conform to community board areas. This change was mandated by the New York City Charter which was adopted by the voters of New York City on November 4, 1975. Referred to as "coterminality," it provides for many of the city's essential services to have similar or coterminous boundaries. As a result of this coterminality plan, most Bronx precincts would be losing area on one boundary and adding area on another. In the Bronx precinct it meant losing some of the quieter areas and adding more troublesome or busier areas. The lieutenant was also concerned about providing figures that would accurately reflect the conditions in the precinct after the change in boundaries. If it was to be done correctly, he explained, it meant getting activity reports on those sectors currently in the adjoining precinct which, after the beginning of the new year, would become part of this precinct. When he posed this problem to the borough office, there was much discussion back and forth about what figures to go with, and when he talked to me about it later a final decision still had not been made. The Bronx was the first borough in which coterminality was to be established with each of the other four boroughs implementing it at six month intervals.

Other officers in addition to the lieutenant ridiculed the notion of using numbers to measure performance. Their arguments were quite similar and put forth with almost the same logic. On the average, according to the New York State Annual Crime Report, there is in New York City a murder every five hours and twenty-five minutes, a robbery every six minutes, an assault every twelve minutes, and a rape every two hours and thirty-five minutes. What, we were asked, do these numbers tell us about the performance of the New York City Police Department? Nothing, was their reply. They only tell us about the performance of criminals. In that same year, officers in the department made 237,311 arrests, up 2.7 percent from the previous year. What do these numbers tell us about the performance of the New York City Police Department? Again, the answer is "nothing." If we assume that the job of the police is to prevent crime, then they argue these statistics tell us only of his failures. Since there are no figures on crimes that *do not occur* because uniformed officers are patrolling the streets, then all crime statistics can do is tell us what the criminals, not the police, are doing.

Concern over police accountability and crime rates is a major problem for police management, particularly in relation to numbers and deployment of manpower. The recent financial crises in New York City have added to the concern and conpounded it because, as a result of first massive lay-offs and subsequent hiring freezes, the size of the patrol force dropped by an estimated 5000 between 1975 and 1977. The idea that there is a discernable relationship between the number of police working the streets, the number of crimes committed, and crime complaints, is not only part of the folklore of policing but is continually used as a budgetary argument by the department. Yet we are also told that the job of policing increasingly is not limited to making arrests and taking complaints. To the detriment of any neat cost-benefit analysis, it includes public relations and any number of other service activities such as taking people to hospitals, giving directions, traffic control, utility problems, landlord-tenant disputes, and guarding visiting dignitaries. Here again this problem is one which is well known to police administrators but, in the absence of any method for establishing comprehensive or even consistent performance standards or indicators, the statistical rate increase or decrease in crime over the previous year or years is continuously employed as the measure of the improvement or decline in the department's or a precinct's performance.

> *Setting Objectives:* Management cop culture attempts to reconcile the demand for greater productivity, efficiency, and responsiveness to the community, with the demand for improved employee relations and working conditions. Street cop culture views these change strategies as trivial, ineffective, and resulting merely in moving lines or boxes on someone's organizational chart.

The field services memo had been quite explicit in directing that "the objective setting process must begin at the precinct level." At first, this seemed a clear acceptance of the importance of local decision making and the setting of authority and responsibility at the same level. As we followed through the actual process, however, a very different picture emerged.

The assigned lieutenant began the process by calling in groups of precinct officers who had specific responsibility for certain performance indicators which had been outlined in the memo. Those fourteen performance indicators were identified under three major headings:

I Serious crime complaints
  • Robbery
  • Burglary
  • Grand larceny auto

II Community participation
  • Operation identification
  • Blockwatchers
  • Precinct community councils
  • Auxiliary police
  • Patrol man hours

III Administration and support
  • New arrest overtime costs
  • Sworn officer sick report manhours
  • Civilian complaints
  • Corruption complaints

- Warrants executed
- Department motor vehicle/scooter accidents

In these meetings, the characteristics to be considered in quantifying each of the performance indicators were discussed and, in some cases, additional meetings were held to work out details of some of the indicators. In other areas, the lieutenant gathered the necessary statistics for the indicators without further meetings. I attended meetings for personnel responsible for the performance indicator areas and interviewed those officers about those "real job" factors which they felt were important considerations for each of the three performance areas in the Bronx precinct, and to get their reaction to this new MBO Program. In the following section I will describe the precinct cop's views of the realities of each performance indicator as they were pointed out to me or as I observed them in operation.

Serious Crime Complaints

In the Bronx precinct for fiscal year 1977 there were 2009 robberies, 4807 burglaries and 1053 stolen cars (grand larceny auto — GLA) reported. These are serious crimes according to the memo, and it is the responsibility of the precinct commanding officer to deploy his manpower to have the maximum influence on the incidence of such crimes as well as other precinct conditions which he may view as priority problem areas. In the Bronx precinct, the commanding officer had organized his patrol force to produce these results in several ways. The regular, uniformed foot and radio motor patrol officers worked in shifts designed to insure that at least the minimum manning level set by the borough command was on patrol at any given time. For radio motor patrol, for example, this meant that there would be seven cars working on every weekday from midnight until 8 a.m. Minimal numbers are set for all other tours as well. On weekends, one additional car was added on the midnight tour. In addition to the radio motor patrol cars, there are also specialized teams, working under the direct supervision of a sergeant, which do not respond to radio calls but perform some specific policing function. One such unit is anticrime, which has twenty to twenty-four plainclothes officers assigned to it. Their vehicles are unmarked and include taxi cabs, vans and, occasionally, even a borrowed postal truck. The anticrime unit has a different shift or tour pattern than regular patrol officers. They usually work either a 10a.m. to 6p.m. (10x6) or 4p.m. to midnight (4x12) shift five days a week with weekends off. Their tours consist of driving throughout the precinct, giving special attention to commercial areas, and seeking out criminal activity such as muggings or robberies which occur on the streets. Frequently, they will spot someone who "looks dirty" and follow them until they either leave the precinct boundaries, or the officers decide that they are relatively "clean, at least for tonight," or until they violate some law that is observed by the officers and are picked up immediately.

The conditions team is another special unit deployed to deal with particular problems or "conditions" that may exist in a precinct. In the Bronx precinct, for example, there were two conditions units, one for burglaries and another for street narcotic sales. Both teams usually worked out of uniform. The narcotics conditions team might send some officers with binoculars to "spot" the street action, either from abandoned apartments or rooftops that overlook high drug sale activity streets or popular drug hangouts. The other team members would be sitting in cars or vans parked nearby, waiting for word from the spotter of some suspicious activity. The spotter radios to the officers waiting below to tell them when they can move in and make the arrest.

While any detail with fixed, regular weekday hours is considered preferable to working around the clock in uniform, anticrime has something of an elitist character according to reports by anticrime officers themselves and by others. We learned in working with anticrime that they tend to see themselves as specialists, in comparison to the uniformed officers who are generalists and must respond to service calls as well as crime complaints. Most of the anticrime officers with whom I spoke said that they did not want to waste their time on "shit calls like the uniformed guys have to handle" and claim that they are being justifiably rewarded for having "shown a lot of activity" while they were in uniform. Since the only activity that such a unit can show is arrests, making "collars" becomes the primary job of these officers. While the existence of quotas is vehemently denied at every level of police supervision, these officers told us quite openly that there are certain quotas they must meet. For anticrime in the Bronx, this has come to mean about four arrests per man a month and "getting on the sheet for the month" is serious business "if you want to keep a good detail." Since anticrime units work as teams, the officers informally divide up arrests. If two of the officers have made arrests for the month and another one of the team members has none for that month, they will see to it that the officer with no arrest gets credit for the next one. Considerable hostility is generated by an officer who steps out of line by trying to "hog" arrests and is not willing to share the work with his colleagues. Other officers will gleefully await their chance to get back at the officer who does so. One well known "hog," for example, left his portable radio in a restaurant and was understandably quite upset when he discovered it missing since he was responsible for this $900 piece of department equipment. His fellow officers arranged with the restaurant owner to hide the radio for a few hours to "put some manners on him."

Whenever we spoke with officers about numbers or quotas, the usual response was that you tried to keep monthly averages about the same from one month to the next because, as one officer explained, "If you show a large increase in arrests during one month, then for sure, the next month the boss is going to want to see you do the same or better." Another officer mimicked one of the bosses: "Don't tell me what you did last month, tell what you are doing for me this month." "Yeh," his teammate added, "and if you didn't get on the sheet for this month, nobody wants to hear about the great arrest you made last month. . . . There's no memory here for good work you did. They only remember the bad stuff." Consequently, one develops the sense, from watching such teams and listening to the cops talk, that what is at stake for the cops is not really the issue of crime in the community or its prevention. The organization of policing seems almost inevitably to create a system where the goal becomes numbers.

As in the case of anticrime, the number of arrests is viewed almost as an end in itself. Units such as anticrime and conditions, whose primary objective is to make arrests and whose sole accountability to the system is based on number of arrests, are critical to that numbers game. Officers on patrol find making arrests both unrewarding and troublesome, since an arrest might involve going to court with all of the attendant frustration of court procedures and delays. The attitude we heard expressed by patrol officers toward arrests is, "We'll take them only if we have to." Another officer explained to us, "It's not like arresting these mutts is doing anything to stop crime. The people around here know that, only they blame us for it instead of the judges and courts. So if there is nothing personally in it for me to make arrests, and it doesn't even keep them off the streets, then you can be damn sure they aren't paying me enough to do anything more." According to officers in the precinct, the only thing that really discourages crime in the precinct is lack of people and businesses as targets, although with coterminality the assumption is that the number of complaints will increase since the areas that will be added to the total precinct are currently the busier sectors of the adjoining precinct.

What can the police officers actually do to prevent crimes from occurring and making neighborhoods or communities safe? A theme we heard again and again is best exemplified by the cop who said, "Nothing we do out here can prevent these bums from committing crimes because they just aren't afraid of us anymore and that's not our fault." Another cop added, "It's just not the same job it used to be, and that isn't because we've changed, it's downtown wants something different from us."

Universally, we heard from cops in both precincts that the problem with rising crime rates was the courts and the attitude of a public that "is more concerned about the crook's rights than the victim." Stories of officers making arrests, often at some risk to their own lives, only to find those arrested back on the streets a few days later were common and told with as much resignation as resentment. "No one really wants us to make arrests, it seems," one young officer told me. "They tell us it costs the department money for overtime and that the court calendars are jammed." He shrugged his shoulders and laughed, "So I really don't understand what they want from us anymore." His partner continued, "With all the restrictions they place on us, it's worth your career to use your gun or put a little muscle on a guy who would just as soon blow you away. We're always the chump, at the disadvantage. Nobody else there backs us up anymore. It's every man for himself."

Another officer said to me that the only numbers activity the department was really interested in was having officers serve motor vehicle violation summonses because "it means money for the city, so we're really paying our own way." Summonses (or "tickets") are usually given for two types of motor vehicle infractions — those having to do with parking illegally ("parkers"), and those for violations involving someone driving incorrectly or failing to obey street signs ("movers"). In the Bronx precinct, there is a civilian employee assigned to maintain records of summons activity. He complained that "the police department is also working for the transit company" since he has to keep a separate account of summonses issued to gypsy cabs working out of bus stops. He explained that the precinct issues approximately 10,000 summonses a year and that "the bosses are always asking for more summons activity at roll call from the men."

Many of the officers hate to give out summonses because they feel that it is demeaning, especially now that there are also meter maids doing the same job. They also have pointed out that one of the reasons that the public feels such resentment toward cops is because most citizens only come into contact with cops when they get a ticket. I met a few cops that had a personal vendetta against certain companies or businesses. For example, there is a gypsy cab headquarters in a store front on one of the main thoroughfares, and one officer complained that invariably the cabs are parked three cars deep into the streets. He gives them tickets every chance he gets "because they are taking away business from legitimate cabs, and guys had to work hard to raise money to buy their own medallions legitimately." Another officer regularly tickets ambulances parked in front of a store front "ambulance service" that, the officer explained, is just a front for a medicaid fraud. The doctors claim the cost of an ambulance, and the "service" is there just in case anyone bothers to check up on them. The officer pointed out a single dilapidated ambulance parked at the corner in front of a fire hydrant, with several tickets stuck under the windshield wiper. Another officer said that he refuses to give out tickets and lets his partner cover for him by writing extra tickets because "I'm just sick and tired of seeing those used car lots with cars double and triple parked into the street, and we're told not to touch them because they pay taxes to the city, while the poor people who live here can't park their own cars on the streets." I was told that at one time, the used car lot owners got together and said they were going to take their business out of the Bronx if the cops did not stop ticketing their cars. "So," the officer concluded, "downtown got the word out, hands off." The CO regularly assigns several officers specifically as "summons men" but it was not unusual to hear an officer go up to the desk lieutenant at the beginning of a tour and tell him that if he lets him work with so-and-so, or puts him in a car instead of on a foot post, that "I'll give you some movers."

A similar attitude and deployment of manpower in the direction of summons activity was present in the Manhattan precinct. The highway safety officer responsible for summons activity there said that he usually figures "one mover to every six accidents occurring in the precinct." He continued, "You're always in competition with your last year's figures and, of course, with the other precincts in your area, because that's what the boss will get pressure about from the borough." When I asked him about the value of activity, his response was, "After all, how can you tell if a man is producing unless you count up something on paper. It's a way of showing that he is doing some work." Another officer commented, "A former captain here made DI [deputy inspector] on the basis of his summons productivity." Some cops in the Bronx apparently had worked out their own system of meeting their summons quotas by getting rid of, or "dumping" their tickets on derelicts, cars that had been abandoned along the street. "After all," one of the officers told me, "it isn't our responsibility if they pay or don't pay, we just have to empty these summons books." His partner added, "You won't believe this, but they found a derelict car that had been issued a couple of hundred summons by the same guys."

"Garbage calls," one officer was saying on an evening tour. "That's all we get anymore. These people use us like we're taxi cabs, and the job doesn't even want us to take care of business out there like we used to do." This officer was expressing an attitude toward the objectives of police work that I heard over and over again in both precincts. The implication was that while there was much, if not more, criminal activity going on in the street, the police's job was being redirected more and more toward service activity, such as responding to ambulance calls, mediating in family disputes or tenant-landlord quarrels, public utility problems, fires, and traffic control. An officer with nineteen years of service, who had worked in several of the boroughs of the city complained, "It used to be if you had a foot post, you knew how to keep that post clean, and the people in the community didn't complain about how you did it. They were just happy that they could walk down the streets safely. Then they started yelling police brutality and so we got the screws put on us. Now the people are yelling again that they want to be able to walk down the streets safely, how can they when the courts turn crooks back out in one day or when we aren't allowed to use our guns to hold some guy." He went on, "Don't talk to me about increases or decreases in criminal activity on these streets. If this job wanted to see a decrease it could be done in no time like we used to handle things, one way or the other, in the old days. Believe me, that's the only way those scumbags learn a lesson."

Community Participation

While the field services bureau plan described community participation as a departmental priority in the memo of November 17, 1977, many of the precinct officers with whom I spoke did not rate any of the performance indicators under this item as being essential to the job of policing. Anything that involved community members in precinct operations was viewed with suspicion and antagonism and summed up as, "They ought to keep the hell out of our business. They just get in our way." While the organization of such programs as Operation Blockwatchers, the precinct community council, and the auxiliary police was the responsibility of several precinct staff officers, most officers saw it as a waste of time that did not involve them and decidedly not "real police work." Although such activity proceeded largely unnoticed by the patrol force, occasionally we would hear complaints such as "The APs (auxiliary police) working out of the Central Park precinct get issued better cars than *we* get for patrol."

The Bronx precinct, however, did have a civilian who had attached himself to the precinct many years earlier and still spends much time in the station house helping with community and precinct activities, such as parties for the local kids at Christmas or Thanksgiving and occasionally raising money in the business community for some piece of equipment that the precinct might need. It seemed that his respect and affection for the men had won the hearts of many of the officers who normally had little good to say for any civilian. Most civilians who like to hang around the station house — derisively called "police buffs" — are considered ludicrous and most cops voiced resentment at the various attempts of headquarters to encourage civilian involvement on the job.

"Cops don't like civilians," was a comment that I heard many times at both precincts. "And especially they don't like them inside the station house where they get to know a cop's business." We were to hear many stories justifying the cop's dislike of civilians and we attempted to come up with some priority listing by frequency of complaints against civilians. The major complaints seemed to revolve around four issues: (1) civilians replace cops in traditional cop jobs, (2) civilians do not understand a cop's job and would tell tales outside the station house without really understanding what had happened, (3) civilians do not have the same sense of loyalty to cops as other cops do, and (4) for a civilian this is just a job, but for a cop it is a career. Sometimes the expression of the "we-they" attitude could be very poignant; once at a precinct farewell party for a retiring cop, the retiree was overcome with emotion at the moment he was asked to speak and could only blurt out, "Only a cop understands what it is to be a cop."

There have been numerous memos, increasing over the last few years, from various command levels advising precinct COs on how to deal with tensions between police and civilian personnel. At the precinct level, the problem mentioned most frequently, was that civilians were replacing officers in jobs previously reserved for officers who had done their time on the streets or are burned out. Several cops working inside were pointed out to me as "retired at full pay." Civilian competency is not really the issue, although this is always questioned in a colorful if derogatory manner. Unfortunately for the civilians who bear the brunt of the resentment, the employee relations section apparently has not resolved the problem of what to do with officers who truly have "done their time on the street," having spent years working round-the-clock, but yet not wanting to retire. It is a problem also for those officers who must hold inside jobs while they are temporarily or permanently on restricted duty.

While there was almost universal hostility toward civilians in cops' jobs, the intensity of feeling expressed in regard to the three other major complaints about civilians varied among the officers with whom I spoke. The fact remains that there is enough concern surrounding each of them to cause continuous and increasing tension between civilians and cops. The cops did not like the idea that topics of conversation by cops on police activity become known to the general public. While I mentioned earlier that it is frequently said that cops are closemouthed and suspicious, I found in fact that in informal conversations around the station house or out on patrol, there is not much that cops will not talk about. "If another cop hears me say I was out of of my sector or stopped in for coffee he knows the job and the dozen legitimate reasons why I might do it, but a civilian just hears 'goofing-off' and he's got no basis for understanding my job and no reason to protect me," explained one officer. Some officers even felt that civilians were all alike in being anticop and that civilian employees feel more akin to, and thus more loyalty toward, a civilian in custody than they would toward the cop who had made the arrest.

In the informal system of relationships among fellow officers, it is much easier for a cop to get back at another cop for a real or supposed wrong within that system. Since the civilian is outside the system it is impossible to use its social sanctions against him. There were a number of instances where civilian employees lodged complaints against precinct cops, and inevitably the cops sided with the officer or officers and showed considerable resentment against the civilian complainant. At such times officers often said that civilian employees were there just for a short period of time and had no real vested interest in their own success and "don't give a shit if they mess up a cop's career."

The fact that civilians have holidays off while police officers do not creates additional hostility since days off, particularly at holiday periods when working means that an officer will not be with his family, are an important issue of work conditions. Officers also complained that civilians are not as dependent on their jobs as cops. On several occasions we heard civilians at both precincts say in front of officers that they would not mind losing their job with the department since they would do just as well collecting unemployment checks. The officers' response was usually that some of their fellow officers who had been laid off for budgetary reasons and were on welfare might like to have those jobs. Departmental supervisors of civilians also express dismay at their lack of actual control over, and their ability to reprimand, civilians since, as one supervisor explained, "The department wants civilianization, so we have to make it work down here but we can't lean on the civilians to get the work done or we get hell from downtown. They don't want to hear our problems. They just tell us to make it work." Another supervisor added, "They keep the best civilians and the prettiest downtown."

While for the most part the civilian employees I observed or worked with kept to themselves, there were civilians in both precincts who seemed to have become fairly well accepted by the officers. The closest relationship involved two male civilian employees who were able to exchange social banter with the cops, talking about female conquests or sports, but as one officer explained, still "minding their own business, not ours." In both cases, the civilians also prided themselves, as they explained it to me, in covering at some time for one of the cops who might otherwise have gotten into trouble. There are also social class and ethnic tensions involved. Much of the recent hiring of civilians has come through federally funded CETA programs and is viewed by many cops as "federal give-away programs for those people who can't find work for themselves," and as evidence of downtown's lack of respect and appreciation for police work: "The job is suggesting that these civilians who were unemployed and supposedly unemployable can do what we have been doing at least as well as we were doing it."

Administration and Support

In an earlier section, I pointed out that with the exception of special units such as anticrime (where high arrest rates lead to increased chances of being kept in this special detail, with its better working hours and conditions), cops feel that a high arrest rate is not helpful to their careers. There is even some feeling that it can be detrimental to one's career since this could suggest to a superior that, in a period of financial crisis the cop is hungry for overtime. A number of cops said that the prevailing work ethic now is, "Don't get involved unless you absolutely have to," or, "It's as bad to do too much as to do too little." Changing administrative procedures in the court system in the Bronx have also significantly reduced time for the booking process after arrest. The overwhelming reaction to this streamlining was antagonism on the part of the officers, who pointed to the financial advantages for an officer making an arrest in Manhattan, or who commented that they were looking for outside jobs now to supplement their salaries since you could not make do with overtime arrests anymore.

One cop's comments to me were typical of others I had heard. "They are looking to cut costs on overtime, but what is our job? Am I supposed to check my watch as I am chasing a guy up the stairs to make sure I won't go into overtime? Who are they trying to kid cutting corners on us out here, when it's business as usual downtown." Once again, what might be viewed as conflicting messages of departmental expectation regarding arrests, is by-and-large interpreted by the street cops as "downtown out to put the screws on us."

Since currently one of the major concerns of police management is cost effectiveness and the reduction of nonproductive time such as sick leave, there is increasing scrutiny here also. The managerial attitude toward the use of sick leave is one factor which clearly differentiates not only precincts but sometimes work units within precincts as well, since taking off sick days can also be a function of the relationship between the supervisor and his men and the morale of a squad or detail. In the Bronx precinct there was a generally more relaxed attitude toward the use of sick leave than in the Manhattan precinct, but even here there has been some tightening up. "It used to be that you could get emergency days off if you had something important to do, or even if you just felt plain shitty or down on that day, but it's getting so hard to get an okay for an emergency day that I just call in sick now and then. They can't say no."

Departmental regulations which are enforced at the precinct, however, make this a risky undertaking. If you are ill, you are supposed to be at home and there are supervisory officers whose task is to check to make sure that officers on sick report are, in fact, at home. Toward the end of the study, the department instituted a new policy for reporting sick. Previously, officers reported directly to the sick desk which then notified the precinct that the officer would not be reporting for work. The officer had to have a police surgeon okay his coming back to work. The officer would usually go to his own physician, then call the police surgeon, who would simply "rubber stamp" him back to work.

The idea behind the procedure was to eliminate the need for going to the police surgeon on minor illnesses. It would allow the precinct administrative officer to call the officer when he first reported and ask if he wanted to put himself back without seeing a police surgeon. A sergeant explained to me two problems that he had with the program. At the administrative level, he had not been able to get any of the desk lieutenants to phone a cop who reported sick to ask if he wanted this new option. He has met with these lieutenants but he feels that they will not use the system for two reasons — because he is "just a sergeant and so they don't like me telling them to do anything since they are lieutenants," and because "those guys never want to try anything new anyway." He also was getting poor cooperation from the men whom he himself had phoned. He said that of twenty calls he had made, only one cop had accepted this method of returning to work. His explanation for this was that when he would call officers who had just reported sick, they would ask if this was some new department policy to save money. When the sergeant said that this was the intention, the response was, "Well, screw them, why should I save them money, I'm going to the surgeon and I'll take a few days."

He also complained about the system of sick time allowed. There is a list maintained by the medical section of officers who are classified "chronic sick." An officer is considered chronic sick if he reports sick more than four times in one year, regardless of the amount of time taken on each sick report. He said that being on the chronic sick list might be detrimental to movement into a special detail or preferential assignment, but in a regular patrol assignment it is no problem to be on that list. He went on to explain that he thinks such a system is a poor one: if an officer feels sick and takes off just one day, that sick report will still count toward chronic sick time; he might as well take a few extra days anyway — it all counts as one time in terms of the chronic sick report limit.

According to departmental records, on an average day approximately 1450 officers (about 5.6 percent of the force) call in sick. Police officers are allowed unlimited sick leave and over the past two years, the average sick leave for each officer has nearly doubled, from ten days in 1975 to nearly eighteen in 1977.

Although the vast majority of civilian complaints against police officers are not substantiated in the investigation which must be conducted on each complaint, the existence of a Civilian Complaint Review Board (CCRB) is a source of great resentment to the police officers I interviewed. This same feeling is apparently widespread in the department, and the Patrolmen's Benevolent Association spent $1 million in 1966 on a publicity drive aimed at defeating the election initiative setting up the CCRB. Here again, the basic police attitude was that only cops can really understand the pressures of a cop's job and that civilians might be biased against policemen and could not therefore render a fair judgment. Mayor John Lindsay wanted to create a review board which would be composed of civilians as well as police officials. The police and the PBA eventually won out. The initiative was defeated and today the CCRB is completely staffed by police department personnel. Attitudes toward civilian complaints and the review process, however, are still strong:

> Anyone can drop a letter on me or phone in a complaint and it will be given to the sergeant for investigation no matter how stupid it sounds and they've got to investigate. If the department is so concerned about efficiency and saving money, how come every idiot who gets his jollies writing letters gets to have his say at our expense? Every complaint, no matter how it is decided, goes into our record.

Other officers complained that the process denied them their civil rights because the civilian making the complaint is not required to appear at the hearing while the officer must appear. It is very easy to get a complaint. A cop's visibility makes him very vulnerable. Once, when I was riding in a radio car on an evening tour, a complaint was phoned in against the officers in the car for having a female civilian (me) riding with them. While there was a certain amount of humor associated with the incident, one of the officers said, "It's always the same old shit, for all they know you were some street walker we arrested or one of your kids was lost and we were helping to find him. But some guy just got a parking ticket, and has it in for cops and saw a chance to give us some trouble. Everybody knows, we're the real second class citizens."

Actually, it seems from our interviews that the police did not so much resent the decisions of the CCRB, which frequently resolved the cases in their favor. Rather, they resented the fact that the department seemed to be encouraging civilians to bring complaints against cops. We frequently heard officers comment, "It's as though they [the department] can come up smelling like a rose if they can just make the cops on the street smell like horse shit." Of 2,409 cases submitted to the board during 1977, 73.3 percent were unsubstantiated, 11.6 percent were substantiated, and 15.1 percent were classified as other dispositions. Officially termed unsubstantiated, 41.8 percent of all cases lacked sufficient evidence to clearly prove or disprove the allegation; 31.5 percent of all cases were unsubstantiated due to the complainant being uncooperative, unavailable, or having withdrawn the complaint. Of the 11.6 percent substantiated cases, 68.6 percent involved excessive use of force, 25.7 percent were for abuse of authority, and 4.5 percent for discourtesy.

The Bronx precinct had shown a significant increase in civilian complaints according to comparative statistics among all precincts for 1977. When I spoke with the CO about this he began by explaining that one of his problems in terms of investigating such complaints is that, if the complaint is submitted directly to the department, rather than to the precinct, he has no way of finding out which officer is involved. He also pointed out that all complaints received about officers working in that precinct are counted toward the precinct total. Unfortunately for the reputation of the precinct, this also includes officers working out of details that are not under the control of this precinct's supervisors, but work out of citywide or borough level commands which are temporarily working within the boundaries of the precinct. Thus a precinct with a sports stadium to which men are assigned from commands all over the city is responsible for, and must include in their total, complaints received by any officer assigned during that event.

Actually, say the cops, the problem is that no one really knows what the number of civilian complaints really says about police performance. One view is that civilian complaints are legitimate complaints of police misconduct and if substantiated should result in some disciplinary measures against the officer. A more prevalent view among the police officers was that in order to accomplish policing ends an officer must be aggressive, even at times taking measures that might be less than gentlemanly. A supervisor much respected in the field by the men as well as by other supervisors, explained that his problem is that he wants his officers to take the initiative and be aggressive, and yet those are the very officers who are difficult to control with "childlike" restrictions, or a book of rules and procedures.

Another supervisor explained that an officer who receives three or more complaints involving force or abuse has his record forwarded to the personnel evaluation section of the personnel bureau, "and they don't know that you can't always reason with the kinds of people we see here." Officers who receive excessive numbers of complaints may be referred to the psychological services unit for evaluation. This supervisor felt that such a departmental policy serves to discourage superior police performance and instead encourages a behavioral pattern of "Do enough to get by but not enough to get noticed." I attended a meeting scheduled by the borough commander to discuss the objectives arrived at by the precinct in response to the MBO memo. At one point the commanding officer of the Bronx precinct explained that given an increase in the size of the precinct boundaries with the introduction of coterminality he would have to project an increase in civilian complaints. He was advised to try to keep the projected increase as low as possible because, "How is it going to look to downtown if it seems we are encouraging civilian complaints?"

Corruption complaints, like civilian complaints, although presented as a field services bureau priority, were viewed by precinct personnel as being a headquarters rather than a precinct problem. One officer explained, "Downtown sees civilian complaints and corruption complaints as a negative reflection on how we're doing our job out here. If I get a complaint I see it as a result of my getting through to one of those mutts out there and because I'm making it hot for him, he wants to get back at me. It's a sad comment on what has happened to this job." He concluded, "The department is taking his side against us." Another officer, in the same context, commented, "I know what my job is out here. The department is supposed to have trained me to do a job. I can't help it if some of the people out there don't like the way I'm doing it. If those guys sitting in offices downtown need to justify their existence by making it rougher for us out here, they have to live with it." He concluded in much the same vein as the previous officer: "I'd just like to see one of those number counters or letter writers come out here for a couple of tours on a hot summer night and see what language he has to use to keep these animals in line."

It is possible that in the past the threat of complaints worried the officers. Our impression over the eighteen months of field observation was that for the most part the officers' reaction was, "So what, what more can they do to us." Particularly in the Bronx, the officers suggested that the worst that might happen would be that they would be transferred to another precinct. "One house is like any other," one officer commented. "The job stinks wherever you are. The only thing that makes it worth it are some of the guys you get to work with." Another officer remarked, "What are they going to do to me, transfer me to a worse precinct? Where could they find someplace worse than the Bronx unless they sent me to Puerto Rico or Africa?"

A lieutenant met at some length with the unit responsible for the execution of warrants in the precinct in order to discuss how to set numerical objectives for warrant execution. (There are two officers regularly assigned to work the warrants unit on a Monday through Friday 7:30 a.m. to 3:30 p.m. tour. The officers use their own car and are not reimbursed for gas or mileage but it is assumed that a good detail is worth it.) From this meeting it was determined that a number of factors impact negatively on the success of warrant service in that particular command. Serving a warrant means finding the individual; that is the first difficulty. In such a high crime, low economic level, community people frequently move. Among Puerto Ricans and other Hispanics, the traditional use of the mother's family name along with (in rare cases instead of) the father's name adds to the difficulty of tracing an individual. The high incidence of buildings destroyed by arson makes it difficult to trace someone through neighbors, relatives, or friends. Building superintendents seldom know or care to know who or where their tenants are, nor are they usually interested in being cooperative with local police. When the precinct turned in its projected activities for warrant execution, they projected a goal of 289 warrants for fiscal year 1977. There were no forms, however, that indicated how this was to be accomplished, whether through increased manpower, more effective use of current manpower levels, or more (or less) supervision.

While the formal discussion of what to do with the warrants squad recognized and documented some of the problems inherent in the system of warrant execution, many more problems existed outside precinct control. They were dismissed without discussion because "those problems are out of our control and the department doesn't want to hear about what we can't do, even if there is a legitimate explanation. It will sound like we are trying to make excuses." It was suggested that these issues be brought up more informally when the precinct CO met with the borough commander to go over precinct figures.

Within the informal precinct social organization, the two officers responsible for warrant execution are generally viewed by other officers as having "a good thing." They choose their own working hours, which have recently been a steady 7:30 a.m. to 3:30 p.m. tour, Monday through Friday. When asked why they choose those hours, the response was that they tried working nights and weekends and did not have any more success at finding people. They also argued that there is more chance of getting someone early in the morning when they might still be sleeping. By noon, one officer told me, "there isn't much chance of finding someone where they are supposed to be or where we could get them." Another frequently voiced complaint was that the forms sent from the courts include descriptive information on the person wanted and a place for a picure — which frequently is not included. "It's very difficult to find a guy if you don't have a picture and the description says a male black, 35 years old, afro, no visible scars on face or body," one of the officers told us with a shrug. "It's an impossible job in a place like this," another officer said. "It just gets hopeless when they keep dumping the warrants on us day after day. We have to log them in, which means hours of paperwork before we can even go out looking."

Apparently, until recently the postal department used to help in locating addresses, especially for changes of address. But with budgetary restrictions and fewer workers, the local post office has been reluctant to take their own time to assist the officers. While the officers persisted in their search for wanted individuals, it was obvious that morale based on some measure of job success was low, but morale in terms of this as an assignment, given the alternative of patrol, was high. Another officer in the Bronx precinct commented about the warrants officers: "They may have it easy because of hours and days off and being able to work out of uniform with little supervision, but it costs them out of their paychecks. They can't make any night differential working steady days, so they pay for it in a sense." One of the warrant officers told us, "The CO pretty much leaves us alone as long as our numbers don't come up too bad in comparison with other commands, and when he can, if there is extra manpower available occasionally he'll slip us a couple of extra men to bring our numbers up."

When we asked those officers responsible whether they felt that the 28 percent increase in warrants executed as projected by the precinct CO was realistic, one of them shrugged and said, "If he gives us more men, then we can get it for him. If he doesn't, then there's no way we can deliver on that number."

In the end, the cops' assessment of the prospects of the MBO plan was right. When the new police commissioner came into office one of the early casualties was this management-by-objectives plan. When I discussed this with one of the administrative officers in the Bronx precinct, he said, "One of the things you learn if you've been on this job long enough is to develop the art of patience: in fact, there is a rule of thumb that says that if they don't get back to you on some directive in two months, you can put it in the dead file because they've either reorganized the office it came out of, transferred the guy who came up with the idea in the first place or changed chiefs. But it isn't gone forever. In a few years someone will dust it off and it will be reborn as a new idea from some forward thinker in the job."

To illustrate the discrepancy between what the management-by-objectives program intended and what actually occurred, we developed an analysis of intended and actual behavior in three areas: the purpose and philosophy of management by objectives, the development of borough and precinct level numerical performance indicators, and objective setting at the borough level.

The Purpose and Philosophy of Management-by-Objectives: Management cop culture can mandate the implementation of new management techniques. They can demand a system whereby numerical indicators of performance are set as the basis for reward or punishment. Street cop culture can corrupt the indicator by working towards making it look good, rather than to measure what it is supposed to accomplish.

What was intended: The management plan described in the memo specifically called for an "objective-based management system, designed to develop specific objectives or standards with which to measure command performance in priority areas of concern; and a management improvement program format designed to assist a command in reaching its Management Plan Objectives through the conduct of specifically programmed activities." Further, that "each command is concentrating its activity under this program on problems *it* has identified."

What actually took place: At the borough and precinct level meetings which described the implementation plans, and in interviews with precinct personnel assigned the responsibility of collecting the data and following through on the request, the major problem areas identified immediately were:

1. Local command priorities had been set at headquarters and there was a strong feeling that they were not necessarily the priorities or areas of concern appropriate to their precinct. Priorities had not, as might be assumed by the wording of the memo, been developed at the local level and passed upward but had been "mandated" from above.
2. The fourteen priority areas had been defined by headquarters. This meant that now not only was it necessary to gather statistics in these mandated areas (some of which were not viewed as problem areas by the command), but areas that were continuous problems locally still must be dealt with at the precinct level.
3. The evaluation and accountability system to be implemented was based upon the number of complaints, recorded warrants executed, RMP accidents, etc. in the previous year, and a projection of the number for the following year, broken down into monthly and quarterly projections. The reaction of precinct personnel was that this type of accountability system, while admittedly simplifying the monitoring process ("for those people sitting behind desks downtown") would be of no help "to us" in identifying or resolving specific problems. In addition, it offered no systematic way of describing patterns to account for problems encountered in attempting to achieve those objectives. It was further noted that this would result in a kind of "contest atmosphere" among the various Bronx precincts with the probable results of a monthly or quarterly listing of precincts by rank according to which command came out closest to their projections, second closest, etc. Thus, there was a feeling that precincts would be judged on how closely they approximated the numerical objectives which the precinct had circumstantially committed itself to, without consideration of any special problems, characteristics, or changing circumstances of the precinct.
4. The management plan in no way took into account the working relationships and social organization of the smaller units that would be responsible for its implementation. What was missing was the most critical assumption underlying management plans such as MBO, that is a mutually agreed upon set of goals and objectives.

The Development of Borough and Precinct Level Numerical Performance Indicators: Management cop culture follows the advice of professional management consultants who simply translate productivity programs designed for business or industry into programs intended to make the "business" of policing more efficient and productive. Street cop culture responds by giving them what they think they want.

What was intended: As described in the memo, "quantification of performance indicators into objectives must involve an analytical process of factors impacting on the performance indicator in question, as well as the programs, resources and activities that may be utilized in order to achieve the objectives. The objective setting process must begin at the precinct level." The memo concluded with the expectation that "the Supplement Objectives when coupled with other bureau-wide objectives contained in the existing Management Plans will result in a more comprehensive, integrated, coordinated approach towards common priority goals."

What actually took place: A careful reading of the above quote would suggest that each precinct should identify those factors which would be important in facilitating or impeding attainment of the performance indicator areas and an outline developed, listing pros (those precinct operations or conditions that favorably affected the achievement of the performance indicator) and cons (those precinct operations or conditions that adversely affected the achievement of the performance indicator). In all of the areas discussed, it was found that a significant number of the factors affecting performance in those areas were actually out of the control of precinct personnel (but not necessarily out of the control of the department). An example was the warrants unit not getting adequate (or frequently even correct) physical identifications or addresses on the warrant forms, and frequently not receiving photos of the individuals to be re-arrested. Such "out of our control" factors, even when the precinct personnel directly involved with the accomplishment of that performance indicator argued that these were exactly the reasons affecting any improvement of performance, were dismissed with the response, "We understand what you are saying, but 'they' will say we are just giving them excuses . . . so we'll have to do the best we can." Thus, the effect was, once again, that the real issues and problems never get sent up through the system. Everyone is too busy trying to read and interpret what the rest of the system wants to hear and not giving them what they should be hearing. We were told by one ranking officer "In this job, they slay the bearer of bad tidings."

1. What was actually done at the precinct to arrive at a specific number objective, was to take the current number of robberies, civilian complaints, warrants executed, etc., and develop percentage increases or decreases which were felt to be achievable and acceptable to "upstairs" and then to present the requested numerical standard based on that percentage increase. What the precinct personnel felt would have been more meaningful as a measure of evaluation for them would have been objectives based on some ratio of, for example, civilian complaints to number of arrests made in the precinct, or number of radio runs, "but we never had any input into the format for objective setting anyway."

2. In the Bronx, the projected coterminality plan was to be implemented within the next two months. Consequently, precinct personnel were aware, of course, that the sector changes involved would, to a greater or lesser degree, affect all of their statistics and consequently affect objectives for each of the performance indicators.

The precinct made an effort to get information on new sectors from the two adjoining precincts and to calculate statistics based on which area would be gained and which lost. When several other precincts complained to the borough of the difficulty of adjusting statistics to take the coterminality changes into account, given the short period of time to prepare their response, borough personnel indicated that precincts could turn in projections based on current boundaries. This was a clear message to the precinct that, "Whose-ever baby this thing was at headquarters isn't going to be around long enough to see it through."

> *Objective Setting at the Borough:* Management cop culture pays little attention to actual police practice, designing new programs and procedures based on seemingly rational and logical factors, while ignoring street level practice that has more impact on day-to-day operations, and the practical outcome of their intended programs. Street cop culture feels increasingly alienated from those so out of touch with the streets.

What was intended: According to the memo, the area commander should be certain in setting objectives that "those objectives should be difficult to achieve but achievable, and that they should be based upon a thorough review of precinct conditions, available resources and alternative programmatic approaches." Also, that in the objective setting conference with the precinct commanders, that the objectives should be "realistic, tough, but attainable," and finally suggested that this conference should be "communicative, not threatening."

What actually took place: At the meeting of the borough commander and several precinct commanders the COs were told to keep numbers at a level which would definitely be attainable. According to these instructions, if the precinct commander felt that he could, for example, reduce robbery complaints by 20 percent, then he should only project a reduction of 12 percent. However, in the area of civilian complaints and radio car accidents, all precinct commanders were told to lower their projections regardless of explanations or justifications (e.g., increased manpower at risk with the additional sectors, higher crime activity areas to be included with the new sectors, etc.), because even if they knew they were going to be high, reporting significantly higher levels of civilian complaints would look like, "we aren't concerned with community relations" or, in the case of RMP accidents, that "we don't care about the well-being of the men." And, wearily, "I know they don't want to hear that." In later discussions the feeling was that the borough commander was "looking over his shoulder" to superiors at headquarters at the expense of local precinct conditions.

1. There was considerable commentary as each precinct commander presented his objectives. This was, in effect, the exercise of peer pressure on those commanders who were projecting very favorable objectives. Quips such as, "Hey, don't make the rest of us look like we aren't doing anything," or, "Where are you stealing the men to do that?" although said in a joking tone, suggested by their consistency and frequency an obvious caution to the other comanders.
2. When the precinct commander responsible for the Yankee Stadium area mentioned special circumstances such as the large number of civilian complaints over which his command had no control, he was told in a manner that stopped further discussion, "Don't worry, we'll handle any problems at the borough level."
3. In a number of cases where precinct commanders had questions and in some cases where the borough commander himself seemed uncertain, someone was sent out to call the field services bureau for clarification. In several of these cases the person called reported that they would have to find the answer themselves and get back to the borough with a reply.

The department's experience in attempting to implement the management-by-objectives program indicates once again the problems of the discrepancy between management cop culture and street cop culture, but there are some important particulars here. While we assumed that headquarters was well intentioned and expected the MBO program to improve efficiency and add acountability at the precinct level, it just as obviously was intended to establish more control over precinct operations. At the precinct level, supervisors as well as street cops ridiculed as well as resented the fact that they were being asked to come up with numbers, which were meaningless to them in terms of actual precinct work. They also pointed out, "They set the priorities that say what's important and we have to give them specifics of how we're going to make those priorities work out here, even if all their priorities don't apply to us." Another frequent complaint was, "As usual, they're in that ivory tower at 1 Police Plaza dreaming up grand schemes without any real idea of what life is like out here today on the streets." We heard many stories and actually observed situations in which numbers were made up for various projected activities in an emprical equation which said, "Promise enough to keep them satisfied, but not so much that you can't live up to what you've projected."

The Blackout

On July 13, 1977, at 9:35 p.m., lights went out throughout the city of New York as a result of a massive power failure. Almost immediately looting broke out sporadically in various parts of the city but was particularly widespread in the Bronx. I was working a 4 p.m. to midnight tour in the Bronx and decided to continue working for the duration of the blackout to help out in an emergency situation for the police, and to observe activity in the station house and in the community. Looting continued throughout the night and into the next day. By the time it was brought under control, loss to businesses as a result of looting and property damage was estimated to be about $135 million. For weeks afterwards there was a continuing debate comparing this blackout with one that occurred twelve years earlier. During the earlier blackout there had been virtually no looting and citizens throughout the city had reached out to help each other out wherever they could. Social scientists, the media, and public officials found a variety of causes for the looting, ranging from frustrations caused by inflation and unemployment in ghetto communities, to a general cynicism and loss of morality in the aftermath of Watergate. The looting also raised a significant public debate over the proper use of police in protecting private property and combating widespread public disorder.

Since the precinct commanding officer was on his summer vacation and the executive captain was not working that tour (both arrived at the precinct later that night), the desk lieutenant had the immediate responsibility for responding to the crisis. An emergency generator was brought out and connected to restore lighting and to maintain radio contact, and radio cars were rushed to major road intersections to control traffic since traffic lights were inoperative. Thirty-eight police officers were on duty at the time. Riot helmets were passed out immediately. Within a half hour of the blackout, officers from other commands began reporting to the station house. A department-wide emergency plan calls for all officers, including those off duty, to report to the precinct nearest to wherever they happen to be at the time of the emergency.

The emergency generator broke down after about ten minutes of use and the precinct was again plunged into darkness until someone found a few candles in one of the offices. As the candles burned lower, a civilian who had been a supporter of the precinct for many years and who frequently helped out in community affairs activities woke up the owner of a hardware store and brought in several cases of candles which kept the station house illuminated until a new generator was brought in at about 2:30 a.m.

Crisis Response: Because management cop culture is effectively divorced from the day-to-day realities of the street it is inevitable that street cop culture can effectively thwart or at least neutralize plans and procedures that have not taken local conditions and organization into account.

As dozens of police from other precincts poured into the station house, supervisors were having more and more trouble organizing and utilizing the increasing manpower. "It's not just enough to have the men," a lieutenant explained. "What we don't have is enough portable radios or radio cars to go around so the extra manpower is useless and most of them are just in the way." Other problems emerged almost immediately. The officers reporting in for emergency duty, most of whom were in civilian clothes, were carrying their off-duty guns rather than their regulation service weapons. There was also concern that if they were put out in the street without uniforms and carrying only their shields as identification, there was the risk of being mistaken for trouble makers since for the most part the cops from different commands were unknown to each other. As officers working in the radio cars began reporting back on the large scale and spreading looting activity in the streets, officers standing around the desk began asking what the bosses downtown wanted them to do about the looters. The bosses, however, were waiting for instructions from a higher command level. Out on the streets the patrol force was also asking what to do and were told to hold tight and wait for further orders. One officer coming in was complaining that they were not getting any instructions over the car radio from communications on who to arrest or what types of locations to cover, and he added, "They're crazy if they think I'm going to break my neck stopping these mutts and then get word to cool it because they don't have the balls downtown to let us handle it." After the first few hours of uncertainty, word came down from the borough that there should be no attempt to use force to stop the looting and that the protection of human life and not private property was paramount.

As the looting spread and some of the stores were set ablaze, the situation became "a nightmare for any supervisor," according to one of the patrol sergeants. "In the first place," he said, "I know how my men feel when we have to pass the word to just take it easy and not let the situation escalate till we have a full scale riot. Downtown doesn't want any newspaper pictures of cops clubbing looters, and I know the guys are itching to break out the baseball bats."

"Our other problem," the commanding officer explained several days later, "was to balance making arrests with depleting manpower on the streets, since the booking process takes time." Another frequently heard complaint was that the cops who had come into the precinct from other commands (because this happened to be the command nearest to them) were not only of little use but actually got in the way. "Extra manpower is useless, unless they come with equipment," one of the lieutenants explained as things began to quiet down during the late morning hours. Another cop laughed as he told the story of watching one of the Manhattan guys trying to do the paperwork on an arrest. "Those spit-and-polish fags from Manhattan don't know how to do real police work, because they've never had to do anything but give out parking tickets." Similar comments were heard frequently in days after the blackout, as the officers began to exchange stories about their experiences during the hours of chaos.

Once the precinct officers had received word from their supervisors that this was a "hands off" situation, and that arrests should only be made if unavoidable, the men appeared to relax, although there was considerable grumbling about appeasement, and comparison of the situation to the Harlem riots of several years earlier. Several hours into the blackout, the level of tension began to lift and it became apparent from quite early on in the emergency that looters were not especially interested in hassling the police but were concentrating on the "pickings." There was some random violence as one officer was shot through the thigh and a brick was thrown through a radio car window, but by-and-large the officers with whom I spoke later in reviewing the event did not feel that there was really any "getting back at the cops" attitude on the part of the crowds or individual looters. One officer came into the station house about 1:30 a.m., and said, "There's something screwy about my trying to break up fights between looters arguing over who got the TV first. I don't know whose side I'm on anymore."

While most store fronts and used car lots were broken into during the early hours of the blackout, there were some store owners who lived close enough to their businesses to come in and stand guard. Officers returning to the station house were commenting that they were more nervous about the store owners using guns against the looters, or anybody they might mistake for looters, than they were about the looters causing violence. "So far the looters aren't using weapons or even being that aggressive," one officer reported early in the blackout. "It seems the feeling is that there is enough to go around for everybody." "The real problem," another officer explained several days after the incident, "was that very early on, the people out on the streets realized that we weren't going to do anything. Sure, some of our guys got even with some of the local boys that have been giving them trouble over the summer. But the guys (the cops) were generally careful because they were afraid that there were cops from other commands around that they didn't know, and even some bosses out of uniform from other commands who might see something and turn in a report."

Means and Ends: Management cop culture has bureaucratized police work in order to make it more easily managed.

Street cops view bureaucratic controls as further confusing and compounding the difficulties they experience in performing their job, rather than assisting them in dealing with the ambiguities and uncertainties.

For some of the cops, the evening's happening was a stroke of luck. Anticrime cops, for example, gleefully claimed that they were "making enough collars to make our quota for the whole month." Others were already counting up their overtime as tours were held over for four hours. Some of the officers lost the extra pay they would make in overtime as they sat around in the upstairs rooms playing cards, waiting to see if they would be kept over. As the long night ended and daylight clearly displayed the massive destruction of whole business sections in the precinct, another reaction began to set in among the officers. As I rode with them over the next few days listening to their stories of the events of that night and the next morning, what began to emerge was a quite clear sense of resentment felt by the cops, not specifically toward the looters, but toward the "system."

The similarity of conclusions drawn about the event by many of the officers with whom I spoke was striking. "What the hell is my responsibility as a cop in all of this mess," was a typical rhetorical question posed over and over again in the following days by the officers who had worked that night. "They tell us it's okay for some guy on welfare to loot a store, but we're supposed to give out summonses to some hard-working guy pushing a hot dog cart because he hasn't bought a license from the city. At least he is working." "It's a joke," his partner added, "I'm supposed to break my ass to protect a guy's property, and then the next day the guy calls into the captain and says to let the neighborhood bums take whatever is left because his insurance will cover the whole thing anyway."

During the long, dark night of looting, frantic storeowners and businessmen called into the precinct demanding protection for their property. By the next morning, however, many of those same store owners came to realize that their insurance would cover any loss. Days later, women and children could be seen picking over the remains in burned-out food stores and clothing stores as radio cars cruised by without stopping. "They talk about pride in our job, in our profession," one cop said with a laugh. "How the hell do those guys sitting up on the 13th floor at headquarters think we feel out here with these animals walking all over us. The whole thing made us look like fools. They're laughing at us, and we're supposed to sit back and take it." "Enforcing the law, that's a joke," one of the officers exclaimed. "I don't think what we are doing anymore has anything to do with the law, it has to do with politics and elections." As we rode around the precinct at daybreak the next morning, the looting was still going on. Cops were standing on street corners next to stores that had been looted, still under instructions not to provoke the looters. By now the frustration and resentment was beginning to show, along with the exhaustion after twelve hours of working. During this time few officers took a meal break. I saw some officers standing outside an appliance store that was being looted simply reach out with their nightsticks and break the picture tubes on the TVs that were being carried past them.

Many of the cops with whom I spoke were alternately enraged and then, increasingly, resigned to the numerous journalistic and sociological analyses and interpretations of the events during the blackout. "Those professors are writing about the looting being caused by resentment against the system, or that they were stealing only essentials like food and diapers. Hell, they were running by me all night carrying stereos, tape decks, and booze. I can't even afford a tape deck." Another officer commented that he was glad to see that everyone was getting ripped-off equally. "None of that soul brother shit we saw during the race riots. This time they were looting and stealing from blacks, from Puerto Rican, and the Jews . . . it was real equality."

An Analysis of the Two Events

What both events serve to illustrate is the conflict between management cop culture, which maximizes administrative processes, juxtaposed to the street cop culture, which maximizes operational pragmatism. In question is the process of change in an organization whose structures, rather than being mutually reinforcing or at best peacefully coexisting, are in competition. The inevitable result appears to be continuous disintegration in communication, morale, and effectiveness, due to the fact that there is no longer a common context for interpretation or action. Instead, each culture (each side) selectively interprets events to justify its own position.

The management-by-objectives event is one example of a management planning technique imported from government and business sectors, and one might argue that there was a lack of fit which led to problems of implementation. A citywide blackout, however, while not an everyday event in policing, certainly represents a class of events which are legitimate and expected in police work. In fact, one of the arguments for tight centralized control in policing has to do with the need to respond quickly and decisively to crisis situations. Yet what we find is that the same disruptive differentiation between street cop culture and management cop culture occurred here. There was a plan to cover this type of emergency, which was quickly put into operation, but when changing situations on the local scene required adjustments to the overall plan, no one at the local level was enpowered or willing to propose adjustments in the absence of direct covering orders from a higher authority. This is not meant to suggest any unwillingness or inability of the supervisory personnel at the precinct to respond competently and quickly to changing emergencies. Rather, there is the ever present concern with "getting burned for acting independently" in any system where authority and responsibility are not equated. One senior ranking officer who had commanded several precincts as well as having held headquarters positions said, "If everything turns out alright and nobody gets hurt and if the newspapers don't make you out to be some kind of a Clint Eastwood character who overreacted, then you get public praise from the mayor and the PC, who point you out as one of the best of the 'finest'! But if something does go wrong, especially if the media picks it up, then they don't want to know you or what you might have accomplished in the past, they'll burn you for not having followed procedures."

What also seemed obvious during the blackout was that the structural organization of the precinct is such that the emergency introduction of new personnel created, at least initially, more chaos than constructive input. To some extent this is explainable by equipment problems but it also represents a measure of the social cohesiveness of the precinct street cop culture and its suspicion of management cop culture. One of the reasons why it was difficult to establish mixed work teams of precinct and nonprecinct personnel was the suspicion voiced by many officers that they did not know personnel from other commands and therefore had no reason to trust them. They might be field associates, or they might be bosses from another precinct, or even headquarters. But fundamentally the problem was that they were not known and so although they were all cops, they did not know what to expect from them nor could they depend on them the way they could in the old days.

Finally, the blackout brought into critical focus the problems of police work in an environment in which social norms and social controls are varied for essentially political reasons. The street cop is placed in a double bind. On the one hand, no matter how justified the political motivation, the officer who sees his job as enforcing the law is placed under the stress which results when an organization presents its members with contradictory goals or purposes. On the other hand, the street cop who has to remain in that community after the emergency often feels he is powerless but nevertheless held accountable in immediate situations where he must be the decision maker.

There is the quality of a game in the present relationship between street cop culture and management cop culture. The headquarters managers can mandate MBO or any planning model but they cannot make street cop/workers treat the new program seriously or honestly. The street cops, on the other hand, can and do fight back with the traditional weapons of alienated employees — foot dragging, sabotage and stealing company time. If the managers do not have the power to require serious acceptance of the planning model, neither do the workers have the power to outwit the managers altogether. What occurs is described by cops as everything from a charade to a race between a three-legged horse and a crippled kangaroo, but in any event, it's all a game. With their perception that not even headquarters took MBO seriously and that everybody knew that it was an "exercise," what happened is predictable. The response is a further attempt to maneuver for position in the contest. Dumping tickets, passing around arrests to whoever needs to "get on the sheet," breaking the picture tube on a stolen TV set, are means of circumventing the formal rules of the game, as are the responses, "You want numbers, we'll give you numbers. You want to treat us like kids, try and catch us." And, "Why should we make you look good, what does it get us?" These clearly denote that while most of them know they cannot possibly win the game, they still want to seek some small victory on the way down.

CHAPTER 7
Implications of the Conflict of Two Cultures for Police Management

What I have described as the two separate cultures of the New York City Police Department is not unique to policing. Rather it is a situation which might be expected in any dynamic, large scale organization in transition. In the case of the NYPD the transition is yet to be completed, and what we have seen and documented is an overlap of the old and the new organization. Now there are two cultures which confront each other in the department: a street cop culture of the good old days, working class in origin and temperament, whose members see themselves as career cops; opposed to this is a management cop culture, more middle class, whose members' education and mobility have made them eligible for jobs totally outside of policing, which makes them less dependent on, and less loyal to, the street cop culture. In a sense, the management cop culture represents those police who have decided that the old way of running a police department is finished (for a variety of external reasons, such as social pressures, economic realities of the city, increased visibility, minority recruitment, and growth in size that cannot be managed easily in the informal fashion of the old days) and they are "going to get in on the ground floor of something new." They do not, like the street cops, regard community relations, for example, as "Mickey Mouse bullshit," but as something that must be done for politically expedient reasons if not for social ones. The management cop is sensitive to politics and public opinion and so will not support a cop like Kelly, whose maverick behavior makes him unpredictable, a potential source of embarrassment. The street cops who are still into the old ways of doing things are confused and often enraged at the apparent change in the rules of the system. So they fight back in the only way they have at their disposal, footdragging, absenteeism, and a host of similar coping mechanisms and defensive techniques. Nor is all of this likely to change soon; the old and the new will continue to coexist for some time because the attitudes, values and ways of doing things have not changed throughout the system.

The emergence of a precinct social organizational model operationalized through the street cop culture and translated empirically into the cop's code is not unique to police organizations. It points to what can happen in organizations when management attempts to provoke change rather than negotiate it. First of all, as in the MBO plan, well intentioned but over-eager police managers have sought to intervene in police work through replacement rather than adaptation. In the replacement method, we attempt to replace inefficient or outmoded techniques with new, more efficient ones. The great technological advances resulting from the scientific and engineering discoveries that have revolutionized agriculture, industry, and medicine provide outstanding examples of this technique. The second technique, adaptation, is more gradual and involves redefining or modifying existing practices. Certainly, there are technological advances that can replace outmoded approaches to policing. Generally, however, we should assume that the major changes needed to produce more effective police work require attitudinal and behavioral changes both in the precinct and at higher administrative levels. This suggests changing the system rather than attempting to change individuals as the only effective means of institutionalizing changes. If relatively permanent (structural) changes are to be brought about, police officer perspectives on policing must also be changed, first to introduce appropriate change in attitudes as well as behavior, and then to maintain support for the changes once they are introduced. Often we speak of the need to achieve a certain climate of sentiment and opinion in order to produce change. Such changes and attitudes are essential but they will not be sustained unless the new ideas or techniques are incorporated in the value systems of the department, or become items on the agendas of both precinct and headquarters levels.

During the course of the study, we met with the head of the Office of Management Analysis in the department in an attempt to obtain departmental approval for an observational study of how policies and decisions flow downward and how requests move through the system. In the course of the conversation, while attempting to demonstrate the importance of such a study, we described to him the futility of the attempt by management to implement the management-by-objectives program. After first indicating that he had not been responsible for, or involved in, designing or implementing that program, he went on to point out that the department knew all along that the MBO program would not be accepted in the field. We asked why, if the department knew that, it went ahead and tried it anyway. He went on to describe quite accurately the negative attitudes held by street cops toward plans emanating from headquarters, but pointed out that there nevertheless would have been some incremental gains from the program.

There is an important reason why I include this story. As so often happens in studying organizations which contain conflicting or competing interest groups, we came away with the distinct impression that what the two cultures of policing say about each other is by and large true. What we are really describing are different perspectives on essentially the same thing, where each perspective is grounded in the situation of the people who hold it. For example, naturally street cops give less weight to what the newspapers say. They do not have to answer to the press or to the mayor. But managers do. In the same way, the managers do not care about the effects of their policy on the daily lives of street cops. They do not have to live with those situations. Any of us would probably do the same thing in either of these positions. While I would argue throughout that it is reasonable for street cops to feel as they do about their situation, this is not the same thing as arguing that it is more reasonable or more correct than the other point of view. The situational nature of the management perspective makes it just as reasonable for them to see things the way they do.

At first, this seemed quite discouraging since, if it did in fact represent the truth, then how could the results of our study do any more than reinforce what each knows about the other? Unwilling to assume that its only benefit would be the more academic one of problem finding, we saw the challenge raised by this police administrator as essentially one which asked, "what is all this going to do for us, since we already know most of what you are going to tell us." For whatever reason, we never received permission for the communications study at the central headquarters level. Consequently, most of what we learned and reported was the result of precinct level observations and interviews. As such, they are not informed by any intimate knowledge of the problems, perspectives, or functions of the higher echelons of the command structure, except to the extent that we heard about management cop culture in the precincts. With this caution, however, there are a few points that can be gleaned from this research relative to departmental interest in improving communications and implementation between headquarters and the field. Research on bureaucratic organizations repeatedly reveals that the intentions of personnel often diverge from those objectives which are formally stated for the organization. Subordinates develop notions of their responsibilities to conform with what they are willing to do. These conceptions may or may not come close to the objectives that those responsible for management had in mind. For the individual this can mean achieving a degree of freedom and autonomy but at the expense of both accountability and the proper function of the system. When the goals of a system are not shared by the people responsible for maintaining the functioning of the systems program, the system is in trouble. One result is that no one really knows what is supposed to be happening in the system, much less what is actually happening.

The principle, which can be stated as, "Individuals seek to maintain themselves as individuals," may be translated into two maxims prevalent in organization theory. The first is that workers are not really committed to decisions they feel they have no part in making. A second is that subordinates attempt to liberate themselves as much as possible from organizational controls. They strive to maintain and even assert their autonomy by hoarding information, supplying inaccurate data, and generally providing only halfhearted cooperation. We believe that what we learned about the social organization of the precinct, the street cop culture in which it finds its values, and the cop's code which operationalizes it, allows us to make some specific recommendations on how understanding and reinforcing the positive aspects of that level of organization can improve both policing and management.

Most of the officers — whether street cops or management cops — described a police department organizational setting in which the upper echelons of administration controlled the setting of objectives, with insufficient consideration given either to the demands of the environment or to the recommendations from the field, even when they were asked for them. The direction of much organizational research clearly indicates that the interface between the operational environment and its contingencies should lead to the key strategic question, "What business are we in?" (Lawrence and Lorsch, 1967). This same literature stresses that organizational controls originating from superiors and conveyed downward to subordinates should be accompanied by a meaningful flow of influence and communication. When control is one-way there tends to be token compliance to the letter of the law, emphasis on the short run over the long run, hiding of infractions of rules, and reduction in subordinate creativity. Accordingly, organizations should seek to open, on a permanent basis, avenues of communication between levels of administration whereby openness is encouraged, real information is transferred, and the system is truly interactive and supportive.

An important point related to the facilitation of information exchange is how it is used. Information forms a basis for analysis which, in turn, provides a basis for evaluation and decision making. It is important that information be used for this purpose, and not for the control of personnel. For example, evaluations should be used as a means of improving methods and premises of operation, not as a mechanism for monitoring and controlling personnel. In this sense a IAD system could be used as a technique to evaluate policies and procedures in the field or of operations in general, rather than as a technique for controling potential misuse of those procedures.

This kind of internal evaluation keeps necessary information flowing from persons who would otherwise feel threatened and so obstruct or neutralize data.

Planning is at the heart of the management function and is essential to the efficient and effective operation of policework. There is virtually no planning at the precinct level where the planning officer is primarily a conduit for statistical information requested by higher administrative levels. As a result, precincts appear to be reactive to whatever situation develops within their boundaries. In actuality, precinct territoriality provides both the precinct and the department with an excellent opportunity for organizational intelligence based on the intimate knowledge which the street cop has of his territory. Conversely, much of the policy and decision making at higher levels of administration are perceived by precinct level personnel as arbitrary and unrelated to local needs and conditions. Further, to the extent that precinct level personnel were not part of the planning and feel no stake in the success of the plan, they will not exert much effort toward the realization of those goals or objectives.

Clearly, if headquarters continues to solicit data from people who are unwilling to surrender it due to their understanding of the personal implications for the bearer of bad tidings, the data supplied will be of questionable value at best. Crozier (1964) points out that, "Those who have the necessary information do not have the power to decide and those who have the power to decide cannot get the necessary information." Information transfer becomes a motivational and a socialization problem and it becomes important to find ways to get personnel to yield their information and generally to gain their trust. This reinforces our emphasis on the need for two-way communications, on the need for personnel to share the objectives that the information relates to, and the need to involve meaningfully all personnel affected by program policies and operations. Decisions should be made by personnel possessing unfiltered information from the level of execution, and the present day realities of policing require that the decision making become a decentralized process and function. Instead of being preoccupied with identifying the decision makers according to who has "legitimate" authority, emphasis is placed on the best possible decision in that situation. Decision making requires adequate information and all too often those in authority simply lack the quantity and quality of information required. Effective decision making also depends on the organizational level at which decisions are made. Different decisions, therefore, are appropriate to different levels.

Currently, and all too frequently, the conflict between these two cultures is characterized by a discrepancy in decisions made at one level, and actions taken on another — based on a different set of norms and values. Actions occur, decisions are made, and things get done, but not necessary in the manner intended by those responsible for the decisions and therefore, ultimately, for the actions.

William James once said that whenever there is a contradiction, it results from the fact that the parties in dispute have failed to make relevant distinctions. Perhaps this is the case here; perhaps police administrators have for the most part stressed problem-solving without first developing a mode of problem *finding*. We may well have failed to ask relevant questions before seeking appropriate answers. Some issues in policing are plain to see; others are less obvious. Some are continuous; others are transient or peculiar to localties. One thing seems obvious: no matter how sophisticated the management system or decision making technology, it stands little chance of producing a meaningful impact on the job if those using it are not aware of the technical, structural, and behavioral problems which plague officers and supervisors at the operational level of policing.

Two common findings in organizational research are relevant here. One of the most persistent problems in organizational decision making is the dilution or distortion of policy directives as they move from central headquarters to the field. The experience is the same in governmental, industrial or military organizations — field units spend a great deal of time interpreting and reinterpreting directives from headquarters, usually to the detriment of their efficiency and morale. Secondly, a number of studies have indicated that an individual's first loyalty is to his immediate organizational unit. The degree to which he sees that unit as representing the total organization is the most important factor in his acceptance of policy and decision making by the leadership. While these two sets of findings may seem somewhat in contrast, they underscore again the importance of understanding the social and behavioral characteristics of the policing environment and the structure and processes on which it is based.

APPENDIX 1
Methodology

Our theoretical orientation for this study centered on the assumption that organized social groups which persist over time are social systems with the character and permanence of social institutions. Our usage of the term "social institution" deviates somewhat from the usual view which is excessively static and structural. Institutions thus are not fixed, monolithic structures, nor are they transmitted across generations as structures. Institutions are the behavioral patterns learned or first established by people seeking to maximize shared values. What becomes institutionalized in this process is not structure in the usual sense — a box containing action — but a code of rules governing social action and defining a pattern of behaviors which are productively efficient in maximizing social and individual gains.

This theoretical orientation goes somewhat beyond the general position of functionalism, as we see the need for identifying some structure of action rather than the usual organizational structure in order to analyze social action. We reject the usual view of structuralists which looks to such positional elements in a social system as "status" or "organization" for structure, finding our structure in the code of rules which illuminates every social system and structures every institution. A social system or an institution is, in one sense, a code of behavior, a structured set of rules of the game which regularize all social action in terms of probabilities inherent in particular social relationships. Our primary research strategy is to gather data on social relations in increasingly larger organizational units by using such traditional anthropological techniques as participant observation over an extended period of time, event analysis, and network analysis. Our contacts, and the field work in general, grow out of natural social settings.

Our scheme of observation, which we call "situational analysis" takes prior observations and concepts into the field and uses them as guidelines for observation. We do not preplan and prebuild an elaborate conceptual framework into which we fit all of the observations. That is to say, we do not build a series of theoretical and conceptual boxes, take these into the field, and fill them with appropriate pieces of action; rather, we go out and observe the social action and then build the boxes in the field as part of the process of the research. In this fashion we are documenting and eventually analyzing ongoing social systems and processes.

It is at this point — looking at policing units as social systems — that we think our study and the field research techniques upon which it is based can be most useful in police management and organizational decision making. These techniques do not assume any preexisting structure and can be used as a means for generating the data for a reconnection between policing environments and organizational structure and function in police work. This is also one of the major reasons for the growing movement to apply the techniques and conceptual methods of field research to criminal justice research. We believe that this study, and a better understanding of the uses of field research techniques in the study of police systems, may help provide better data on how the police organization functions, as well as serving as a tool for developing models for organizational change in a department. Police work, whether it occurs in formal or informal settings, tends not to repeat laboratory models — if indeed they will submit to satisfactory model building at all. There are moments of action and response, fluid and sometimes nonverbal, as well as routine moments and inactivity. Although their caprice can be overstated or overdramatized, the events of day-to-day policing do manage to trouble even the most precise comprehensive research strategies, as anyone who has attempted observational studies of police work will attest. Nonetheless, conventional research and evaluation procedures in police work continue to exploit arbitrary environments, statistical measures, and "problem" approaches in seeking data about what goes on in police/citizen, police/police, police/supervisor encounters and in building knowledge of policing process and structure.

Anthropology offers considerable expertise in traditional organization or systems research in this regard. One distinction of anthropological inquiry is that it describes "natural" environments and "ground-level" behavior. The descriptive activity of anthropology concerns "actual" behavior or what people are observed to do, not simply "normative" behavior or what people say that they are doing or claim ought to be done. The confusion between normative and actual behavior is an important one in police research and practice. In a sense, the problem of relevance in law enforcement practice may be viewed as a failure to recognize the inconsistencies, contradictions, and paradoxes police confront daily in trying to make sense of differences between actual and normative behavior. Further, the tendency of traditional police research to generalize and attempt applications of findings from questionnaire responses or departmental statistics to natural environments and real behavior is much less a tendency of the past than much of the current technically impressive research reports and "sophisticated" analyses of data would have us believe.

The data upon which this study is built derives from a long-term field study of two police precincts using the approach just described. Specifically, we looked at a precinct as a social unit which operates according to an observable code of rules which control and regularize behavior. Control systems of this sort begin with values which define what is "good" and what is "bad," what is expected and what is condemned, what is tolerated and what is not tolerated. Ultimately, however, social behavior in the precinct is guided by specific social rules which attempt to operationalize these values and apply them to everyday situations. Thus, while group values give us some general sense of what is expected, it is the social code which states what actions will be approved and which will be condemned by other members of that social system. We felt that we could define the optimal social and behavioral structure for the precinct by observing, recording, and analyzing these rules.

APPENDIX 2

Research Plan

To carry out the proposed research, we planned to select one New York City police precinct for an in-depth field study over a period of eighteen months. During the last six months we planned to look at a number of other precincts as well, in order to develop some insight into the generalizability of our major findings. Our field experience convinced us that a comparative study of two precincts would better serve this objective. As a result we spent fifteen months studying one precinct and three months studying a second precinct.

Throughout the eighteen months of field work, a member of our research team worked with the various units operating at the precinct level and with patrol and other operational units who daily police the community, observing everyday behavior and interaction. We used a number of established anthropological techniques in the field: participant observation (becoming as much as possible, given the researchers' civilian status, a member of the precinct community and observing on a daily basis what takes place), event analysis and network charting or observing some incident in the precinct (whether it was a critical incident or routine), tracing the networks of individuals involved in the incident, and then developing descriptions of how the incident is perceived or responded to by those involved.

This use of event and network analysis is based upon the analysis of three major behavioral components: (1) the social-behavioral field, (2) person-to-person contacts, and (3) social relations sets. Essentially, this means that in the first few months of field work we map the behavioral environment of the precinct and conduct preliminary interviews with a sample of precinct members. It was during this period that initial contacts were made which paved the way gradually to their acceptance of the researchers and of the overall purpose of our study. We were, in effect sponsored in the

131

precinct by those officers we had first established contact with, and through whose networks of informal social relations we were gradually introduced into the social system. Our daily field presence involved working full eight-hour shifts in the complaint room taking reports, as well as riding as observers in radio cars during duty tours. Initial contacts and introduction into the working life of the precinct allowed us to develop site-specific strategies for data collection and preliminary analyses. Through these preliminary observations and interviews we were able to develop an index of events and activities which allowed us to focus on and select those planned and unplanned events which we felt were crucial to understanding social relationships, social controls, and shared meanings and understandings among precinct members. We then developed a purposive sample of events and activities, and of precinct members who formed informal networks surrounding and resulting from these events which collectively described the social system of the precinct.

Our research plan of action was:

1. To obtain an overview and descriptive baseline data and to identify the actors, processes, and activities in the precinct and at various supervisory or command levels. These data allowed us to establish sequential sampling procedures for further interviews and for the development of site-specific strategies for data collection and preliminary analyses.
2. From these preliminary observations and interviews, we developed an index of events and activities during the first months of field work which allowed us to focus on planned and unplanned events and activities in the precincts. Throughout our field research we observed and analyzed the operations of the precinct and specific activities. We were observing and analyzing leadership behavior, patrol performance, control strategies, social and occupational processes and interactions, officer/officer transactions, supervisor/officer transactions, administrative-organizational systems processes, and to the extent that they were observable within the precinct, headquarters and community influences on personnel, work, and attitudes.

There were a number of specific practices within the generic technique of participant observation which we used. One technique was to follow an officer or team throughout the day. This meant riding as an observer in radio cars on full tours as well as working and observing in specialized activities such as anticrime units, warrant serving units, detective squads, community relations, etc. While the actions of the officers we were observing were the primary foci of observation, their social interaction, patterns of approach and avoidance, and other transactional processes were also apparent through this process.

Prolonged observation of a single team or special unit was also an important technique. Our previous police research experience, and the fact that we were able through prior contact to establish the critically important social acceptance within the precinct which permitted at least a minimum degree of unobtrusiveness, were highly important. Observing the social and behavioral dynamics of single units within the precinct provided a continuity of social action not possible in observing only sporadically or sequentially in a number of units. It is this type of in-depth qualitative study which distinguishes ethnographic approaches from sample-oriented survey techniques.

The variety of interactive combinations of occupational and social action in the precinct offered an opportunity to comment on a variety of situations, modes of work performance, age and sex differences, and ethnic diversity. While it was not of course possible to observe every possible permutation, our presence on a daily basis for eighteen months provided a unique opportunity for gathering observational data and interview material about policing and policemen.

Since the basic research design of the fieldwork portion of this study was based upon anthropological techniques, data analyses were an integral part (rather than a later stage) of the continuous methodology. The process was one of sequential analysis of data. The analyses took place in three stages:

1. *The selection and definition of events, concepts, and indices.* Here the first stage of the analysis began in (a) seeking out those events and activities for observation which promised to yield the greatest understanding of the social and occupational significance of precinct organization, and (b) looking for items which might serve as useful indicators of the more difficult questions of how such events or activities are organized into the ongoing life of the precinct. The simple analytic conclusion of this stage of sequential analysis is that a given phenomenon exists or that two phenomena were observed to be related in one instance; the conclusion says nothing about the frequency or distribution of the observed phenomenon.

2. *The check on the frequency and distribution of phenomena.* In this second stage of sequential analysis, the field team had gathered many provisional problems, events, concepts, and indicators, and the analytic problem now was one of determining which of these was worth pursuing as major foci for study. This was done through continual comparative analysis of the data. Thus the fieldworker determined if the events that prompted the development of these provisional indicators were typical and widespread in the precinct and how these events were distributed among categories of people and organizational subunits.

3. *The construction of models of structures and codes of rules defining the sociocultural context of precinct structure and organization.* The final stage of analysis consisted of incorporating individual findings into

a generalized model (or models) of the social organization of the precinct and the codes of rules which were identified in step two of the sequential analysis scheme.

It is generally assumed that the problem of validity is greater in interviewing than it is in participant observation because the data are one stop removed and one is observing through the eyes and perception of other individuals. In this study, validity checks on interview information came from a process in which we measured the internal consistency of interview data and sought verification of information through other sources wherever possible. Since we were also involved in the process of observation, some of the data could also be checked against our own observations.

The question of validity and reliability is one which is common to field work studies. Our solution was to establish a standardized system of assessing both the validity of the data which we were recording and the reliability of the source of a particular piece of data and how much validity to assign to the information which he is passing on from someone else and about which the analyst must make a separate judgment; an informant who is unreliable may pass on a piece of information which can be checked against factual data such as departmental records (which may or may not be accessible to the researchers). Because we felt that the questions of informant reliability and data validity had to be looked at separately, we set up a two dimensional system for assessing data. Assuming that the closer the field worker is to the data the more certain he is of what he is seeing and hearing, we assigned the highest validity score to those data gathered where at least one fieldworker was present during the action being reported. Where we were not involved as direct participants, we assigned lower validity scores to data gathered by interviewing informants and coded interview materials into one of three categories according to how carefully we were able to check the data. Data which could be checked against standard, available documented sources — complaint reports, precinct statistics and so on — received the highest score, and where the data came from one source only, we assigned the lowest score.

Since we were constantly comparing data as they were gathered, we also began building up a profile of how reliable our major informants were. Here again we assigned the informants to categories: "always reliable," where information from that source was consistently accurate in terms of factual checks or subsequent interviewing; "usually reliable," where the data usually but not always checked out; "reliability unknown," where we had been unable to check; and "unreliable," where later checking indicated that the individual seldom provided accurate information. The following table indicates the reliability/validity coding scheme which was applied to all data used in analyses for the study.

	VALIDITY SCORE		**RELIABILITY SCORE**
A.	Data gathered through observation with direct participation	1.	Informant always reliable
B.	Data gathered through observation but not as direct participant	2.	Informant usually reliable
C.	Interview data checked against documentary or other factual source.	3.	Reliability of informant unknown
D.	Interview data corroborated by one or more additional informants	4.	Informant unreliable
E.	Interview data from a single informant		

Once we had assigned both a reliability and a validity score to interview data we combined the two into an index number and used only those units of data which had a reliability-validity index of D-2 or above for analysis and summary reporting.

Since our interest was in finding and describing the networks and rules by which members organize their universe and behavior, our problem in analyzing the field data was one of formulating both networks and rules. Our approach was essentially that of developing a natural history of the areas of behavior in which we were interested, what is generic about the behavior of members of these networks in these areas, and how did they explain this regularity. Since we were continuously coding observational and interview data into categories for analysis and constantly comparing the behaviors we sorted into a particular category, we began formulating tentative networks from the very beginning of the research. As new data came in we reexamined networks, adjusted them when necessary and developed tentative rules for aspects of behavior within the network. Once we had identified a tentative rule of behavior, we would compose a maxim which described how a member of the network should behave under a given set of circumstances. We would then express the maxim to members of the network as something we had observed in order to see if they recognized it. When we were satisfied that our formulation of a particular network or set of behaviors was sufficient to allow us to make the judgments and perform the action in the way which members of a network would consider appropriate, we added the rule to our code of rules and noted any exceptions.

Bibliography

Ahern, James F., *Police in Trouble: Our Frightening Crisis in Law Enforcement*, Hawthorne Books, Inc., New York, 1972.

Angell, John E., "Toward an Alternative to the Classic Police Organizational Arrangements: A Democratic Model," *Criminology*, 9, American Society of Criminology, Sage Publications, Beverly Hills, California, 1971, 185–206.

Astor, Gerald, *The New York Cops: An Informal History*, Charles Scribner's Sons, New York, 1971.

Baehr, M.E., Furcon, J.E., & Froemel, E.O., "Psychological Assessment of Patrol Qualifications in Relation to Field Performance" (Law Enforcement Assistance Administration Project #046), United States Government Printing Office, Washington, D.C., 1968.

Banton, Michael, *The Policeman in the Community*, Tavistock Publications, London, 1964.

Barnes, J.A., "Class and Committees in a Norwegian Island Parish," *Human Relations*, vii, 1954, 39–58.

————., "Networks and Political Process," in M. Schwartz (ed.), *Local Level Politics*, Aldine, Chicago, 1968.

Barth, Frederick (ed.), *Ethnic Groups and Boundaries*, Little, Brown and Co., Boston, 1969.

Bayley, David, & Mendelsohn, Harold, *Minorities and the Police*, Free Press, New York, 1969.

Becker, Howard S., *Outsiders: Studies in the Sociology of Deviance*, The Free Press, Chicago, 1973.

Bion, W.R., *Experiences in Groups and Other Papers*, Tavistock Publications, London, 1961.

Bittner, Egon, *The Functions of the Police in Modern Society*, National Institute of Education, Chevy Chase, Maryland, 1970.

————., "Policing Skid-Row: A Study of Peace-Keeping," *American Sociological Review*, 32, October 1967, 669–715

Black, Donald J., "Police Encounters and Social Organization: An Observation Study," unpublished Ph.D. dissertation, University of Michigan, 1968.

137

Blau, P.M., *The Dynamics of Bureaucracy*, University of Chicago Press, Chicago, 1955.

————., *Bureaucracy in Modern Society*, University of Chicago Press, Chicago, 1955.

————., *Exchange and Power in Social Life*, Wiley, New York, 1964.

————., "Comparative Study of Organizations," *Industrial and Labor Relations Review*, Vol. 18, 323–38.

————., *On the Nature of Organizations*, Wiley, New York, 1974.

Bordua, David J. (ed.), *The Police: Six Sociological Essays*, Wiley, New York, 1967.

Cooper, Terry L., "Professionalization and Unionization of Police: A Delphi Forecast on Police Values," *Journal of Criminal Justice*, 2, 1974, 19–35.

Crozier, M., *The Bureaucratic Phenomenon*, University of Chicago Press, Chicago, 1964.

Dawson, Peter, "Social Mobility and Stress Affecting Officers," *Police Review*, December 6, 1974.

Denyer, T., Callender, R., & Thompson, D.L., "The Policeman as Alienated Laborer," *Journal of Police Science and Administration*, Northwestern University School of Law, Vol. 3, No. 3, 1975.

Diskin, S.D., Goldstein, M.J., & Grencik, J.M., "Coping Patterns of Law Enforcement Officers in Simulated and Naturalistic Stress," *American Journal of Community Pathology*, Vol. 5, No. 1, 1977.

Durner, J.A., Kroeker, M.A., Miller, C.R., & Reynolds, W.R., "Divorce, Another Occupational Hazard," *The Police Chief*, IACP Inc., Gaithersburg, Maryland, November 1975.

Ellison, K., & Genz, J.L., "The Police Officer as Burned-Out Samaritan," *Law Enforcement Bulletin*, March 1978.

Fox, James & Lundman, Richard, "Problems and Strategies in Gaining Access in Police Organizations," *Criminology*, American Society of Criminology, Vol. 12, No. 1, University Park, Pennsylvania, 1974.

Gaines, L.K., & Ricks, T.A., *Managing the Police Organization*, West Publishing Co., New York, 1978.

Garmire, Bernard L. (ed.), *Local Government*, Police Management, Washington, 1977.

Goldstein, Herman, *Policing a Free Society*, Ballinger Publishing Company, Cambridge, Massachusetts, 1977.

Goldsmith, J., *Police Community — Dimensions of an Occupational Subculture*, Palisades Publishers, Pacific Palisades, CA, 1974.

Haas, E., & Drabek, T., *Complex Organizations*, MacMillan, New York, 1973.

Hahn, Harlan (ed.), *Police in Urban Society*, Sage Publications, Beverly Hills, California, 1971.

Ianni, F., *Culture, System & Behavior*, Science Research Associates, Chicago, 1967.

————., "Ethnic Succession in Organized Crime," Summary Report, National Institute of Law Enforcement & Criminal Justice Publication, Washington, D.C., 1973.

————., "Attitudes Towards the Relationship between Stress Relief and Youthful Drug Abuse in Two Recent Field Studies," *Drug Use in America*, National Commission on Marijuana and Drug Abuse, March, 1974.

————., "Social Organization of the High School and School Violence," in Wenk et al, *School Crime and Disruption: Prevention Models*, U.S. Department of Health, Education, & Welfare, Washington, 1978.

Ianni, F., & Reuss-Ianni, E., *A Family Business: Kinship and Social Control in Organized Crime*, Russell Sage, New York, 1972.

————., *The Crime Society: Readings in Organized Crime and Corruption*, New American Library, New York, 1976.

Katz, D., & Kahn, R.L., *The Social Psychology of Organizations*, Wiley, New York, 1966.

Kaufman, Charles N., "The Danger Within: Organization Stagnation," *FBI Law Enforcement Bulletin*, February, 1973.

Larson, Richard C., *Urban Police Patrol Analysis*, Massachusetts Institute of Technology Press, Cambridge, 1972.

Lawrence, P.R., & Lorsch, J.W., *Organization and Environment*, Harvard University, Graduate School of Business Administration, Boston, 1967.

Lefkowitz, Joel, "Psychological Attributes of Policemen: A Review of Research and Opinion," *Journal of Social Issues*, Vol. 31, No. 1, 1975.

Levi, L., & Anderson, L., *Psychosocial Stress: Population, Environment and Quality of Life*, Spectrum Publications, New York, 1975.

Levinson, Harry, *Organizational Diagnosis*, Harvard University Press, Cambridge, 1972.

Lotz, R., & Regoli, R.M., "Police Cynicism and Professionalism," in *Human Relations*, Vol. 30, No. 4, 1972.

Lundman, Richard J. (ed.), *Police Behavior, A Sociological Perspective*, Oxford University Press, New York, 1980.

Knapp, Whitman et al., *Report of the Commission to Investigate Alleged Police Corruption*, Braziller, New York, 1972.

Manning, Peter, *Police Work: The Social Organization of Policing*, Massachusetts Institute of Technology Press, Cambridge, 1977.

————., "The Researcher: An Alien in the Police world," in Arthur Niederhoffer and Abraham Blumberg, *The Ambivalent Force*, Dryden Press, Hinsdale, Illinois, 1976.

Manning, Peter, & Van Maanan, John, *Policing: A View from the Street*, Goodyear, Santa Monica, California, 1978.

March, J.G., & Simon, H.A., *Organizations*, Wiley, New York, 1958.

McAdoo, William, *Guarding a Great City*, Harper and Brothers, New York, 1906.

McGrath, J. (ed.)., *Social and Psychological Factors in Stress*, Holt, Rinehart and Winston, Inc., New York, 1970.

McGregor, D., *The Human Side of Enterprise*, McGraw-Hill, New York, 1960.

McLean, A., *Occupational Stress*, Charles C. Thomas, Springfield, Illinois, 1974.

McNamara, John H., "Uncertainties in Police Work: The Relevance of Police Recruits' Backgrounds and Training," in David Bordua (ed.), *The Police: Six Sociological Essays*, Wiley, New York, 1967, 163–252.

Meyer, J., & Rowan, C., "Institutionalized Organizations: Formal Structure as Myth and Ceremony," *American Journal of Sociology*, 83, 1977.

More, Harry W., Jr., *The American Police, Text and Readings*, West Publishing Co., St. Paul, Minnesota, 1976.

Muir, William K., *Police, Streetcorner Politicians*, University of Chicago Press, Chicago, 1977.

Nicholas, Alex, *Black in Blue: A Study of the Negro Policeman*, Appleton-Century Crofts, New York, 1969.

Niederhoffer, Arthur, *Behind the Shield: The Police in Urban Society*, Doubleday and Co., Inc., Garden City, New York, 1967.

Niederhoffer, Arthur, & Blumberg, Abraham, *The Ambivalent Force*, Dryden Press, Hinsdale, Illinois, 1976.

Olson, B.T., "Police Opinions of Work: An Exploratory Study," in J.R. Snibbe and H.M. Snibbe (eds.), *The Urban Policeman in Transition*, Charles C. Thomas, Springfield, Ill., 1973.

Punch, Maurice, *Policing in the Inner City*, Archon Books, Hamden, Connecticut, 1979.

The President's Commission on Law Enforcement and Administration of Justice, *Task Force Report: Police*, Government Printing Office, Washington, D.C., 1967.

Radano, Gene, *Walking the Beat*, World Publishing Co., Cleveland, Ohio, 1968.

Radzinowicz, S.L., & Wolfgang, M.E. (eds.), *Crime and Justice, Volume II: The Criminal in the Arms of the Law*, Basic Books, Inc., New York, 1977.

Reiss, Albert J. Jr., *The Police and the Public*, Yale University Press, New York, 1972.

———., "Police Brutality — Answers to Key Questions," *Trans-action*, Vol. 5, No. 8, 1968, 10–19.

Rubinstein, Jonathan, *City Police*, Farrar, Straus, and Giroux, New York, 1973.

Ruchelman, Leonard (ed.), *Who Rules the Police?*, New York University Press, New York, 1973.

Savitz, Leonard, "The Dimensions of Police Loyalty," in Harlan Hahn (ed.), *Police in Urban Society*, Sage Publications, Beverly Hills, California, 1970.

Shelter, Leonard, *On the Pad*, New York, 1972.

Sherman, Lawrence W., "Middle Management and Police Democratization: A Reply to John E. Angell," *Criminology*, 12, 1975, 363–77.

Silberman, Charles, *Criminal Violence, Criminal Justice*, New York, 1978.

Simpson, Anthony E., "The Front Line of Defense: The Future of Policing in America," a guide to bibliography and theory, unpublished manuscript, New York, 1978.

Skolnick, Jerome H., *Justice Without Trial, Law Enforcement in Democratic Society*, Wiley, New York, 1966.

Skolnick, J.H., & Gray, T.C., *Police in America*, Educational Associates, Little, Brown and Co., Boston, 1975.

Stahl, Glenn O. (ed.), *Police Personnel Administration*, New York, 1974.

Stoddard, Ellwyn R., "The Informal 'Code' of Police Deviancy: A Group Approach to Blue-Coat Crime," *Journal of Criminal Law, Criminology, and Police Science*, Northwestern University School of Law, Vol. 59, No. 2, 1968, 201.

Symonds, Martin, "Emotional Hazards of Police Work," *American Journal of Psychoanalysis*, Vol. 30, No. 2, 1970.

————., "Policemen and Policework: A Psychodynamic Understanding," *American Journal of Psychoanalysis*, Vol. 32, No. 2, 1972.

Taylor, Angela, "Women Police Officers," *The New York Times*, November 2, 1974.

Thibault, E., & Weiner, N., "The Anomic Cop," paper prepared for presentation at the 68th Annual Meeting of the American Sociological Association, August 27–30, 1973.

Tifft, Larry, L., "The 'Cop Personality' Reconsidered," *Journal of Police Science and Administration*, Northwestern University School of Law, Vol. 2, No. 2, 1974.

Ulberg, C. & Cizancks, V.I., "Motivation, Effectiveness, and Satisfaction," in O. Glenn Stahl, and Richard A. Staufenberger (eds.), *Police Personnel Administration*, Washington, D.C. Police Foundation, 1974.

VanMaanen, J., *Pledging the Police — A Study of Selected Aspects of Recruit Socialization in a Large, Urban Police Department*, U.S. Department of the Navy, Office of Naval Research, 1972.

Vernon, Robert, "Systems Analysis in Contemporary Police Management," *Traffic Digest and Review*, April–May 1969.

Walker, Tom, *Fort Apache*, Crowell, New York, 1976.

Westley, William, "Secrecy and the Police," *Social Forces*, 34, March 1956, 254–57.

————., *Violence and the Police*, MIT Press, Cambridge, Massachusetts, 1970.

————., "Violence and the Police," *American Journal of Sociology*, 59, July 1953.

Williams, Robert, *Vice Squad*, New York, 1973.

Wilson, James Q., *Thinking About Crime*, Random House, New York, 1975.

————., *Varieties of Police Behavior: The Management of Law and Order in Eight Communities*, Antheneum, New York, 1974.

Index

OAKTON COMMUNITY COLLEGE

DES PLAINES, ILLINOIS 60016